CW01084425

THE GOLD MAN FROM THE EAST

Nobu Sue

Published by Subon Publishing

Hardback colour ISBN: 978-1-7384544-0-2
Paperback black and white ISBN: 978-1-7384544-1-9
E-Book ISBN: 978-1-7384544-2-6

Cover Art: Lauren Frances—www.instagram.com/labhrai
Book Design: www.ShakspeareEditorial.org

To my Daughters, Airi and Eri who endured the writing of this book, during their adolescence, with grace and wisdom beyond their years

The Author—Nobu Sue
photo © Odette Sugerman

Contents

PREFACE

The 2008 global financial crisis was planned. It did not happen by accident. It was easy to plan it, the difficulty was how to remove the evidence of the plan so that nobody would know.

Most books on the subject do not go far enough, they stop short of pointing the finger in the right direction. This includes government reports and enquiries.

This book is not just about the crisis itself, it's about the victims who were targeted and used to clean up the evidence. The waste product was sold to Taiwan and the garbage disposal men (and women) were ABN AMBRO Bank, Royal Bank of Scotland and RBS Sempra.

ABN AMBRO was purchased by RBS in 2007 for this purpose and RBS Sempra was created in June 2008 by Royal Bank of Scotland and JP Morgan Chase, in a joint collaboration.

The reach and mandate of these garbage disposal people was far-reaching, interfering with and altering public announcements and even reports published by financial commissions. Central Bank policies were altered to allow access, by anything which could loosely call itself a distressed asset, to free money.

This caused distortion of the money supply and unsolvable inflation, which impacted greatly on the global 99%. Of course, the obscenely super-rich 1% got richer.

Assistance from the Kuomintang political dynasty in Taiwan was essential for the cleanup to work. Coincidentally (or not) the strategy also assisted the embezzlement and exportation of Chinese and Taiwanese assets by the KMT.

It was the perfect solution to the greatest financial scam in history. A win-win or, as the Chinese would say, Shuang Ying, for the rich and powerful forces that planned and executed the global financial crisis.

This book will give a fresh perspective on the subject. It asks the hard questions which others have shied away from.

In addition, the book will show how Royal Bank of Scotland used a Greek shipping company to destroy one particular victim, to prevent him from exposing what was going on.

The victors of WWII now rule the world and are still invading and conquering, either directly or indirectly. Divisions and alliances have been formed, factions, opposing interests, conflict, destruction. Yet all of us live on one planet, with finite resources.

If one of us takes too much, more than we need, another must go without. Understanding the truth about 2008 is to understand our descent into a future Armageddon.

Yet, despite the facts presented in this book and the solutions offered, ultimately, readers must ask their own questions – and form their own conclusions.

GLOSSARY

I am aware that the financial terms used in any book of this nature may not be fully understandable to every reader. I have tried my best to explain such terminology in everyday language as I write—without interrupting the flow of the narrative. I hope this glossary will also be a useful tool in negotiating the financial-speak, so I've placed it at the front of the book rather than at the end, for convenience.

AIG, American International Group: An American insurance company bailed out in 2008 because of reckless sales of Credit Default Swaps (CDSs) and other risky insurance products.

Bear Stearns: Wall Street investment bank purchased by JPMorgan Chase after its failure in 2008.

Baltic Dry Index: A shipping and trade index created by the Baltic Exchange (London) that measures changes in the cost of transporting raw materials.

BHP Billiton: The world's largest mining company, based in Australia and London.

Big Bang: The deregulation of the London Stock Exchange and the City of London by the Thatcher government during the 1980s.

Big Short, The: A book and movie about the financial crisis and how the CDS market was shorted. Spot the name of the restaurant in the last scene—no relation!

BIS, Bank for International Settlements: An international organization for the cooperation of central banks and international monetary policy makers.

Chapter 11: Form of bankruptcy that involves a reorganization of debts, usually filed by a company that needs time to restructure its debts.

Clarksons: World's largest shipping brokers who oversee and orchestrate contracts between charterers and ship owners, while also functioning as an investment bank for the shipping industry.

CDO, Collateralized Debt Obligation: A promise to pay investors cash from payments of interest and principal on loans. The mortgage or loan is the collateral. "The engine that powered the sub-prime mortgage boom." A CDO can contain a range of loans (car loans, credit cards, mortgages, etc.).

CFTC, US Commodity Futures Trading Commission: Its given mission is to foster open, transparent, competitive, and financially sound markets.

CMO, Collateralized Mortgage Obligation: Unlike a CDO this will only contain mortgages.

Commodities: Raw materials or primary agricultural products that can be bought and sold, such as copper or coffee.

Commodity Market: Soft commodities, like wheat or sugar, or hard commodities, like oil or iron ore, are traded on commodity markets (i.e., a soya milk manufacturer in England can buy a bulk delivery of soya beans from Argentina). However, this kind of physical trade is less common than a purely financial trade in which investors buy and sell futures. For investors it is simply a way to make a profit and, while they might technically own a future crop of wheat, they'll always sell it on before delivery is due.

CRA, Community Reinvestment Act: A law designed by the US Federal Reserve to encourage banks to lend to low- and moderate-income neighborhoods.

CPFF, Commercial Paper Funding Facility: an institution created by the NY Federal Reserve to provide liquidity to US issuers of commercial paper; one of the many funding initiatives in response to the financial crisis of 2008.

CDS, Credit Default Swap: A financial contract where the buyer of a debt (mortgage) buys an insurance from the seller in an effort to eliminate possible loss from default. CDSs are unregulated and anyone can buy them, even if they don't own the underlying loan, so they quickly become another betting tool.

Currency Swap: Involves the exchange of interest (and sometimes principal) in one currency for the same in another. It is a foreign exchange transaction and

doesn't need to be shown on a balance sheet; is usually used to hedge long-term investments.

Depository Bank: A specialist financial entity for stock transfers and agency services in the USA and for trading services in the EU.

Derivative: A contract or product whose value is linked to (or derived from) the performance of an underlying entity, such as an asset or an interest rate. Most are traded over-the-counter (off exchange), but others are exchange-traded derivatives (ETDs) that go through specialized derivative exchanges. The three main investment instruments are: stocks (equities & shares); debts (bonds and mortgages); and derivatives.

Dodd-Frank Act 2010: In the aftermath of the 2008 financial crisis the Dodd-Frank Wall Street Reform and Consumer Protection Act of 2010 (Dodd-Frank Act) enhanced the CFTC's regulatory authority. On 8 June 2017 the House of Representatives voted to replace sections of it with the Financial CHOICE Act.

DJIA, Dow Jones Industrial Average: one of the world's most watched stock indexes.

Due Diligence: Investigating a potential investment to confirm all the facts—such as reviewing financial records and so on.

Exposure: Market exposure represents the amount an investor can lose from his/her investments, should things go wrong. The greater the investment volume, the greater the exposure, the greater the risk

Fed, Federal Reserve: The Central Banking System of the USA, similar to the Bank of England in the UK. The New York Fed can print dollars, as its special function.

FCIC, Financial Crisis Inquiry Committee: This US Commission was created to "examine the causes, domestic and global, of the current financial and economic crisis in the United States" as part of the Fraud Enforcement and Recovery Act (Public Law 111-21) passed by Congress and signed by the President in May 2009. It ceased to exist on February 13, 2011.

FOMAC, Federal Reserve Open Market Committee: A committee within the Federal Reserve that manages the buying and selling of government bonds. It makes key decisions regarding interest rates and it controls the supply of money.

FICO: A credit scoring company in the USA that measures consumer credit risk and adds credit "scores," similar to credit agencies in the UK like Experian and Equifax.

FCA, Financial Conduct Authority: A UK independent financial regulator created in 2013, when it replaced the FSA. It has the power to investigate suspected financial crime and ban misleading financial products.

FSA, Financial Services Authority: Independent UK financial regulator, abolished in 2013 following the financial crisis of 2008, replaced with the FCA.

FFA, Forward Freight Arrangement: Ship owners and speculators use FFAs to hedge against the volatility of freight rates. A ship owner can sell the price of using one of their ships for a future date and therefore protect against the risk of the price falling. An FFA is a derivative product, similar to a CDS.

Front-running: This is when an investor uses inside information to make a profit on the stock or commodities market. Traders and firms will do this through undisclosed and unregulated bank accounts.

Futures: Financial products obligating a trader to buy or sell something at some time in the future, recording the quality and quantity of what's to be bought or sold and the agreed price.

Glass-Steagall Act: This legislation describes four provisions of the US Banking Act of 1933, separating commercial and investment banking.

GRG, Global Restructuring Group: Division of RBS responsible for aiding failing businesses, helping them to meet and continue their loan repayments.

Hedge Fund: The purpose of a hedge fund is to generate high profit for its clients. They are less regulated than other investment vehicles and require a large minimum investment to join. The term hedge comes from the investment style, which is to hedge risk by holding both long and short positions. They use pooled funds and are aggressively managed.

IBAN Code: This is an international banking account number in a standard numbering system that identifies bank accounts around the world.

ICAP: Now known as the NEX Group plc. A UK-based business focused on post-trade risk mitigation and electronic markets. TMT was ICAP's largest customer in 2007.

IFRS (International Financial Reporting Standards) vs GAAP: One of the major differences lies in the conceptual approach in which US GAAP is rule-based, whereas IFRS is principle based. However, IFRS includes guidance that could easily be considered as sets of rules rather than sets of principles.

Insider Trading: Illegal buying or selling by someone who has access to information (specialist knowledge that is not public) that will benefit the trade.

IPO, Initial Public Offering: The first time the stock of a private company is offered to the public—often used by smaller, younger companies seeking capital to expand.

IRS, Internal Revenue Service: The USA's tax collection agency that administers the Internal Revenue Code enacted by Congress.

Lehman Shock: Lehman Brothers, the world's third largest investment bank, filed for Chapter 11 bankruptcy and was immediately bought by Barclays and Japan's Nomura Holdings for little or nothing.

Leverage: The ratio of a company's total debt to the value of its total assets. The greater the amount of debt, the greater the leverage.

Leverage-to-Equity-Ratio: A financial measurement in which debt is compared to assets. It assesses a company's ability to meet its financial obligations.

Libor: London Interbank Offered Rate is the primary benchmark for short-term interest rates around the world.

Li's Gaussian Copula Formula: A mathematical formula used by financial institutions to price CDOs, which were previously too complex to price.

Liquidity: A measure of the amount of cash (or assets that can be quickly turned into cash) available to an organization to meet its obligations.

LCH, London Clearing House: A clearing house that helps to orchestrate a trade between two traders by guaranteeing the settlement of the trade and therefore taking on the risk should one of the traders default. In 2008 it was indirectly owned by the London Stock Exchange.

Long, Long Position: Buying stock or commodities or currency with the expectation that the asset will rise in value, which the investor normally has no plans to sell in the near future. Hence, "buying long", the opposite of "short."

L-shaped Recession: A type of recession and recovery that resembles an L on a graph, showing a sharp decline, followed by a long period of stagnant growth.

Margin Call: An investor buying or selling positions will use a margin account, which must always contain a minimum amount of collateral to pay off any losses. A broker (like RBS) will make a margin call if that amount falls below a certain percentage of the whole investment portfolio. If the investor refuses to pay the margin call, then the broker/bank has the right to liquidate the portfolio and put the money into the margin account.

Market Rigging: When some of the companies in a market act together to stop the market operating as it should in order to gain unfair advantage (e.g., price rigging to artificially inflate prices).

Moral Hazard: (In the context of this book) Lack of incentive to guard against risk, where a bank is protected from the consequences of that risk (by government).

MBS, Mortgage-Backed Securities: An umbrella term that includes CDOs and describes any financial product that uses mortgages as an asset.

OBS, Off-Balance Sheet: Financial activity that is not on a company's balance sheet. A way of hiding a company's level of debt and liability that is allowable under current accountancy rules.

OTC, Over-the-Counter: A trade conducted directly between two parties, other than through an exchange like the NYSE or the LSE. Each participant quotes the price at which they're willing to buy or sell a security. Unlike the stock market, there is no definitive price list, so you never know if you're paying too much or selling for too little. OTC markets are not well regulated and are used by traders for bonds and derivatives.

Quantitative Easing: If a central bank needs to increase liquidity and spending in the private sector without increasing the inflation rate they create money electronically and use it to purchase securities, commonly government bonds, from financial institutions.

Pledged Asset: A pledged asset (e.g., shares) is transferred to a lender to secure a loan. It can be short or long term, hence "short pledge document."

Ponzi Scheme: A fraudulent investment scam promising high rates of return with little risk. Generates returns for early investors by recruiting new investors. Eventually, there isn't enough money to go around and the scheme unravels.

Preferred Stock: Having a priority claim on dividends

over Common Stock (i.e., preferred stockholders get paid first).

PDCF, Primary Dealer Credit Facility: After the collapse of Bear Stearns, the Federal Reserve initiated PDCF in March 2008, so that financial institutions could sell securities through a "discount window" for funds in the form of a repurchase agreement (repo loan). It was intended to pump liquidity into the overnight loan market that banks use.

Reganomics: The economic policies of the Ronald Regan administration in the USA, especially with regard to the promotion of unrestricted free-market activity.

Repo 105: An accounting trick in which a company classifies a short-term loan as a sale and uses the cash to reduce its liabilities.

Rights Issue: An entitlement to shareholders to buy additional shares directly from the company, generally at a discount to the current market price.

RBS, Royal Bank of Scotland: One of the subsidiaries of The Royal Bank of Scotland Group plc, together with NatWest, Coutts Bank, Citizen Bank, Ulster Bank and RBS Securities. The largest bank in the UK, 70% of which is still owned by the government.

Royworld Express: RBS' own payment system—a bit like Western Union. Usually used for small payment amounts.

SCP, Synthetic Credit Portfolio: unit created in JPMorgan Chase to lower risk by hedging against the potential losses of other JPMorgan Chase trades.

Section 13(3): A controversial part of the Federal Reserve Act which gives the Fed the emergency powers to provide liquidity to anyone it likes, whereas they are usually restricted to loaning money to commercial banks.

Securities: Financial instruments that hold value, such as ownership of a stock or bond or option. A means of raising capital—equities (stocks and shares) or debt (CDOs and CMOs).

SEC, Securities and Exchange Commission: An independent financial regulatory body in the USA that oversees the securities industry and stock exchanges.

SFO, Serious Fraud Office: A specialist prosecuting authority in the UK to tackle top level serious or complex fraud, bribery and corruption. Part of the UK criminal justice system covering England, Wales and Northern Ireland, but not Scotland, the Isle of Man or the Channel Islands.

Shadow Banking System: Unregulated financial activities taking place outside the scope of regulators, carried out by investment banks, mortgage brokers, hedge funds and other sources of credit. Also unregulated activities carried out by regulated institutions. A kind of financial black market.

Short-Selling: Usually we invest in something because we believe it will rise in value. Short-sellers invest in financial instruments on the basis that they'll lose value because they've been overvalued. A short-seller will borrow a security from a lender, but doesn't have to return the exact same security, just a security of equal value. The short-seller then sells the security he/she borrowed and buys it back when it loses value and returns it to the lender. They profit from the difference between what they sold the security for and what they bought it back for. Short-selling is viewed by many as immoral and "shorting" can affect the markets.

Special Purpose Vehicle: Is a subsidiary company whose obligations are secure even if its parent company goes bankrupt. It can also be designed to serve as a counterparty for CDOs and other derivatives so any financial risk is isolated and doesn't cause too much damage—it is also a convenient way for financiers to hide debt.

Stocks and Shares: Securities that signify ownership in a corporation and represent a claim on part of the corporation's assets and earnings.

Stress Test: Computer-generated simulation models to determine the financial health of an organization through the reactions of asset and liability portfolios to different financial situations.

Sub-prime Mortgage: A mortgage issued to a borrower with a low credit rating. They carry higher interest rates than conventional mortgages. Sub-prime refers to the credit score of the borrower.

SWAP: A derivative contract through which two parties exchange financial instruments. Most are interest rate swaps and are not traded on exchanges, but are over-the-counter (OTC).

SWAP Agreements: A policy created to allow central banks to provide currency directly to foreign countries during the international credit crisis and is still practiced today. Example: the European Central bank sells a set number of euros to the Federal Reserve for dollars at the current market exchange rate. The ECB will buy back their euros at an agreed date at the price they sold them. In the meantime, the ECB will loan their dollars to banks and corporations who want to do business with America.

Swift Code: To identify banks and financial institutions around the world and used for money transfers between banks.

Synthetic CDO: A CDO that bets on the performance of another CDO. If I buy a synthetic CDO, I'm betting that the original CDO won't default. If it does default, then I owe the investment bank I bought it from a lot of money. Complex synthetics take bets on other synthetics. One of those complex financial products where few people knew what the underlying asset was worth and one of the causes of the 2008 financial crisis.

TARP, Troubled Asset Relief Program: A US government program to purchase toxic assets and equity from financial institutions to strengthen its financial sector. Signed into law on 3 October 2008 to address the sub-prime mortgage crisis.

Teaser Rate: A starting rate on an adjustable rate mortgage (ARM). Usually below the going market rate and issued to entice borrowers. It soon grows to the full indexed rate.

Toxic Asset: Any financial asset whose value has fallen so greatly that the owner can't sell it on at a satisfactory price. After the financial crash, some people found that their houses were toxic assets.

Tranche: A portion of a debt (CMO or CDO) with a unique risk. An AAA tranche inside a CDO would be low risk, whereas a B tranche would be high risk.

TCM, Treasury Cash Management Account: An account that allows you to manage your cash transactions through one portal. It acts as an umbrella or main cash hub under which all your investments flow in and out.

TSLF, Term Securities Lending Facility: Set up by the Federal Reserve to allow primary dealers to borrow Treasury securities on a 28-day term. Another of the many facilities set up in the wake of the 2008 financial crisis.

US GAAP, General Accepted Accounting Principles: Although most countries have now switched to IFRS.

VIX Index: Volatility index, shows the market expectation of 30-day volatility and often referred to as the "investor fear index."

VLCC, Very Large Crude Carrier: An oil tanker designed for bulk transport of oil.

VLOO, Very Large Oil and Ore Carrier: Variation of the VLCC. It can switch from oil to iron ore.

Volatility: A statistical measure of the amount of uncertainty or risk. High volatility means the price of a security can change dramatically over a short period of time in either direction, which leads to market instability.

Volcker Rule: A US Federal regulation that prohibits banks from conducting certain investment activities with their own accounts. Its purpose is to prevent insider dealing and front-running.

WTO, World Trade Organization: The global organization governing the rules of trade between nations. Its function is to help producers of goods and services, importers and exporters, to protect and manage their businesses. Largely responsible for globalization.

Zombie Bank: A bank that has a net worth of less than zero, but continues to operate because it is backed by government and taxpayers.

PROLOGUE

THE SET-UP

It's Monday May 7, 2007, 9:00am. My secretary Cecilia briefs me on my schedule in the chairman's office on the eighth floor of the Today Makes Tomorrow building in Taipei. Floors two to eight are fully occupied by the TMT Group—we're expanding rapidly. I'm informed of three ladies in the waiting room with no appointment. I agree to see them. They're smiling and elegantly dressed and I assume they're from another of the private bankers who regularly visit us in Taipei.

One of the ladies introduces herself as Neena Birdee, from the Royal Bank of Scotland in the UK. The other two are from RBS Taiwan and RBS Singapore. They've brought gifts of playing cards and golf balls and mah-jong sets, all bearing the RBS logo. I smile, is it Christmas?

It is for them.

The ladies sit at my conference table and Neena Birdee explains why she's here.

'Royal Bank of Scotland is the largest bank in the world and we'd like to do business with a shipping tycoon like yourself.'

She's very confident.

I reply, 'How nice. In what way can we do business?'

Shipping is a service industry. We carry goods to make our money. I provide a service for my clients, it's what I've done all my life.

Neena Birdee continues, 'We want to help you with your trading, and there's no need to do KYC.'

KYC means know your customer and is the process of verifying the identity of clients and is used for anti money-laundering regulations. The ladies smile in unison.

'Just open an account, that's good enough to start with.'

Neena Birdee is friendly and reassuring. TMT already does business with many domestic and international banks, so why not with "the largest bank in the world"? I'm flattered.

'OK.'

She immediately produces a form and signs it, not quite on the dotted line, which I don't notice at the time. Another form is already signed as "Prime Brokerage." She leaves the bank's signature blank on both forms. Why does she sign this way? Is it preplanned? I don't ask. At that time I don't know about the Prime Dealer Credit Facility that will enable RBS to get US Federal Reserve money. I assume it's a standard document, so I make the biggest mistake of my life and sign it too. Neena Birdee then produces a pile of other documents and puts them on the conference table.

'You can read these later.'

It's quick. It's sharp. I'm suckered! Then they leave. It's the last time I'll see her until 2014.

That 30-minute meeting begins my ten-year nightmare.

At the end of November 2007 I get a call from Royal Bank of Scotland. There's a man on the telephone shouting and demanding a $48 million margin call. I'm puzzled, our forward freight arrangement (FFA) positions are healthy enough. The man on the phone isn't prepared to listen.

'If you don't pay today, your company will get a bad name in the market and you won't be able to trade.'

What can I do? I pay up immediately. The next day the same thing happens—another $48 million. We're very busy and $45 million comes back quickly, so I assume it's just an accounting glitch and it'll sort itself out. What I don't know is that Royal Bank of Scotland bought Dutch bank ABN AMRO in October 2007 for more than it's worth. The purchase leaves RBS short of capital, so they're using my money to solve their short-term liquidity problem, to the tune of $103 million.

I'm using an independent shipping broker called Mattia Besozzi for TMT's FFA trades. He calls me and says BHP Billiton, the world's largest mining company, is willing to trade with us "as much as we want." This comes out of the blue and I'm curious.

'Why?'

Mattia replies.

'I don't know.'

But he does know. I'm not aware that Mattia is front-running my FFA trades (using the information for insider dealing) with others because TMT trades are big enough to influence the markets. Neither am I aware that the Royal Bank of Scotland is worried that I might stop doing business with the bank because of the erratic margin calls. They're beginning to manipulate me into a position where I can't leave them, by setting up a conspiracy of option calculation mistakes, incorrect margin calls and general confusion, between themselves, Clarksons shipbrokers, BHP Billiton and rival shipping companies like Petros Pappas' Oceanbulk.

I'm told by Royal Bank of Scotland that a man called Gerard Joynson will be handling my account with them. He turns up at TMT's London office in Cavendish Square in April 2008. He looks serious.

'We forgot to charge you $58 million for option trades.'

'What?'

'We want the $58 million we forgot to charge!'

I'm stunned. I don't know what he's talking about as the bank's already withdrawn $58 million. How can a bank forget to charge for a whole month's trades? He continues to demand the money, so I ask him to show me the contract. This request silences him. He has no contract. He gets up and leaves the TMT offices. I don't see Gerard Joynson again until February 2010, but I remember his face.

It's May 2008 and I'm visiting London. As usual it is part business and part holiday. I'm meeting with businessmen, playing golf and eating spaghetti bolognese, my favorite Italian food, which they do particularly well in England.

I'm strolling through Cavendish Square in the late morning on my way to Royal Bank Of Scotland's headquarters in Bishopsgate to meet Gerard Joynson, who works exclusively on my account. The meeting's been scheduled to discuss the $58 million London Clearing House charges that the bank "forgot" to debit for a month, something that seems quite unlikely to me. But I'm sure there's a simple explanation and I'm confident we can sort the matter out quickly and amicably.

It's bright but unseasonably cold and I'm wearing a thick woollen scarf I've borrowed from the hotel concierge. Summer feels like a long way off. I've no idea, as I saunter down the tree-lined avenues in holiday mood, that my meeting with Gerard Joynson will be hijacked and the topic will be something I'm totally unprepared for.

I've never been to the RBS offices before but, from the outside, they're exactly what I expect; a grandiose construction of glass and chrome, jutting into the sky like the prow of an impressive warship.

I enter the reception and am directed upwards by a lone receptionist half-heartedly picking at a Tupperware salad. She doesn't ask me to sign in, which seems very strange. As I leave the elevator, I'm surprised to find that the whole floor is deserted. My footsteps echo as I walk, somewhat nervously, past rows and rows of empty desks and abandoned computers. It seems like the workstations have been suddenly deserted, as if there's been a fire drill or something. The computer screens are still operating and wisps of steam drift up from half-drunk cups.

Finally, a man dressed in black pokes his head out of an office and beckons me inside. He sits at the end of a big table and the room is full of folders and paper documents, as if it's some kind of bunker or interrogation room—very strange for the head office of a bank, dour and dismal, without even carpet on the floor.

The man has a long face and a shock of white hair that sits awkwardly on the top of his head—it looks coarse and slightly askew, like a wig. I try hard not to stare, but the man, who introduces himself as Gerard Joynson's boss, seems completely nonchalant. He looks like Joynson—the same facial structure—and I think to myself, maybe they're related?

Gerard isn't present.

The man sits with his back to a window, through which the spring sunshine is streaming and casting him into silhouette. He tells me to sit and, when I ask him where everybody is, he says they must be at lunch. I can't think of any office in the world, let alone a top global banking headquarters, that would be completely abandoned during the day, even if it is lunchtime?

I'm not offered tea or coffee or refreshment of any kind, not even water. Ignoring my attempts at polite conversation, the man immediately begins asking me a series of quick-fire and bizarre questions about myself and my experience with RBS. Questions he should know the answers to and which seem quite irrelevant to me.

'Where are you from?'

'Taiwan.'

'What is your business?'

'Shipping, of course.'

He wants to know how often I check the accounts, how much I currently have in margin calls, and whether or not I would ever consider moving my company's accounts to another bank.

As I've said, my company is Today Makes Tomorrow, a shipping business, and Royal Bank of Scotland is supposed to be handling FFAs for us. But this man doesn't mention FFAs, nor the London Clearing House options which the bank "forgot" to charge to TMT—which is the reason I'm here. There's nothing in the conversation that's remotely connected to Gerard Joynson and his handling of my account.

He speaks slowly but erratically, trying to hide his accent. When I don't answer his totally unexpected questions immediately, he appears to become a little impatient, narrowing his eyes and pursing his thin lips as he leans back in his ergonomic chair and assesses me coldly over the top of his steepled fingertips.

After about half an hour of this strange inquisition, he stands up and dismisses me without extending his hand.

'You can go now!'

The floor is still eerily empty when I leave the room.

The man never introduced himself nor presented me with a business card, so I don't know who he was. In hindsight, maybe I should've been more inquisitive, but I'm grateful for having a major Western bank looking after my company interests, without which I wouldn't be able to trade FFAs through the London Clearing House.

Nevertheless, it's not how I expected to be treated, especially by someone who purports to be nothing more than a mid-level manager at RBS. I'm being courted by companies all over the world who want me as an investor or an advisor. This man, by contrast, wouldn't even shake my hand. I wondered why he'd taken such a dislike to me. Was it something I said? Maybe the way I stared at his hair? Perhaps I delayed too long in answering his questions?

On the way back to my hotel I reflect on my behavior, but can find nothing that might be construed as discourteous in any way. Oh well.

About a month later, I'm invited to Royal Bank of Scotland's headquarters in Bishopsgate again—again to meet Gerard Joynson. And, once again, Gerard isn't there and I meet his strange lookalike—this time the man appears different, smiling and dressed in a blue suit. Once again, he asks me a series of probing and unremitting questions that leave me feeling slightly dazed, as if I'd just been embroiled in some Kafkaesque trial. When we finish, he dismisses me curtly again.

'You can go now!'

In June 2008 Royal Bank of Scotland is overexposed to the US sub-prime mortgage crisis, it's paid far too much for ABN AMRO, just to stop Barclays from getting its hands on that company, and it's had to raise £12 billion from shareholders in the form of the biggest rights issue in European history. At this time, the writing is on the wall and RBS is literally insolvent and desperately needs liquidity. My shipping business, Today Makes Tomorrow, has plenty of liquidity. In other words, RBS needs my money to save it from oblivion.

Today Makes Tomorrow is RBS' largest individual private client, with a vast amount of wealth for the bank to plunder. I'm a very successful man. Nobu Sue is a name to be reckoned with in the global shipping business, and in financial circles in general, especially in the East. I use private jets, stay in the best hotels, always get the best table in the best restaurants. In short, I'm a flamboyant, jet-setting, man-about-town.

I'm also very naïve when it comes to the chicanery of Western bankers.

Today Makes Tomorrow is the perfect victim for Royal Bank of Scotland. We're privately-owned, exist outside Western regulatory oversights and, as an Asian company, we have no "friends" to protect us from the vultures in the City of London and on Wall Street. The man in the wig and blue suit knows I'm not a member of the "Old Boy's Network" that controls the financial sector and he realizes that, while I'm an expert in the shipping industry, I'm inexperienced when it comes to the dirty dealings of high finance.

I'm stepping into the jungle of investment banking and the predators are starting to circle—but I can't hear their growls of greed.

And so, after my sinister meetings with the strange man on the deserted floor of RBS' headquarters in Bishopsgate, I resume my visit to London, marveling at the white, Portland stone alcoves of Temple and the Monument's golden flame as I stand at the top of Lombard Street and take in the grandeur of the colonnaded Bank of England. It's a place of financial elegance, of historical dominance and prestige. So easy for a man from the East to become overawed!

Little do I know, as I merrily take in the sights and sounds of London Town, that the predators hiding in the financial undergrowth are already upon me and my TMT shipping company.

And so, after ten years of investigating what really happened, I'm writing this book. The true story of the world's largest financial scandal that you probably won't have heard of—yet. I'm not a professional writer and I'm trying to keep the story as simple as possible, despite the complex financial transactions involved. So please bear with me, and anything that's not fully explained will be dealt with in subsequent books that I plan to write.

The man in the blue suit

TODAY MAKES TOMORROW

My father's name was Chin Wun Su and he set up the Taiwan Maritime Transport Company in 1958. With a single secondhand ship he started transporting bananas to Japan, because Taiwanese bananas were the best in the world and the Japanese people loved them. It was a small, family-run business with only one kind of cargo and two ports to sail from to Yokohama, Keelung and Kaohsiung. I spent a lot of my childhood exploring the docks and playing games with the ship's crew. They'd hide bananas for me to find and I soon developed a keen sense of bearing and an encyclopedic knowledge of the ship's nooks and crannies. I loved being there. I loved the smell of salt water drying on the hull and the pungent fume of fuel as the propellers began to churn, drowning the shouts of the sailors. Shipyard docks were, in my young eyes, always alive with adventure.

In those days the ports weren't as busy or bureaucratic as they are now. There were times when a boy like me could just sit with his feet in the water and listen to the stories told by the sea-captains and sailors. It was a magical place for a child to grow up, full of different voices and languages, smells and sounds. But nothing stays the same forever and I started to get older, sitting in on business discussions and decision making, while also getting an education at Keio University in Tokyo. As my father's business continued to expand he progressed from shipping just bananas to wood chips and grain, and from one ship to many. I continued to learn and, by the time I was a young man, I knew pretty much everything there was to know about the shipping industry.

Shipping makes the world go round, it has done for thousands of years. Maritime merchants carried spices and furs to the courts of ancient kings and conquerors. And, although the cargoes might have changed, it's still the ship that brings most of the fruit and vegetables to our local supermarkets. Over 70% of the earth is covered by oceans and over 90% of world trade is carried out by the international shipping industry. We might not be as aware of the many bulk carriers and containers and reefer vessels in the same way as we're aware of the airplanes flying overhead or the lorries grunting down the highways, but they're out there nonetheless.

My father died in 2001 and I took over the business. The shipping market was depressed after 9/11 because of the fear factor; uncertainty meant that fewer people were trading and it took a while for things to heat up again. But globalization was on the move and gaining momentum, spreading in directions no one could have predicted, and people needed more ships than ever before. The Internet had survived the collapse of the Dot-Com bubble at the birth of the new millennium and, soon, buyers and sellers who had been relatively remote from each other only a few decades previously, could do business from all over the world at the click of a keyboard. Chances were, they'd need my ships to collect and deliver the merchandise from and to their front doors. The signs of an economic boom were beginning to show themselves in India and China. One of those signs was China and Taiwan joining the World Trade Organization (WTO); that's when I knew things were going to get busy.

The great uni-controllers of China were going, that ambivalent line from ancient dynasty to Marxist mediocrity dissolved in the waters of pecuniary necessity. The new leaders were accountants, not dogmatists, budget men and investment bankers and entrepreneurs. The global labor pains of the millennium gave birth to a new bundle of joy and brought a hungry market force into the world. The Chinese were building a vibrant economy on a bustling manufacturing base, fueled with a cheap workforce. The old bogey of China's human-rights record was being trampled into the dust of the Wild East boomtown that everybody wanted a piece of. Lowest crime rates in the world were due to the Chinese's natural respect for authority. There was a creative buzz in the air.

The global market opened up from West to East. China had, for a long time, been a sleeping giant and the way to help the Western financial system recover from the losses of the Dot-Com crash was to wake it up! So that's what the financial establishment did. Under my stewardship Taiwan Maritime Transport became a major player in the transportation of grain and iron ore as soon as China began its grand sweep of industrial purchasing, through the early years of the millennium in preparation for the Olympic Games in 2008. TMT became a global business and I renamed it Today Makes Tomorrow, keeping the original initialism.

I'd grown up surrounded by shipping, just like a fish grows up surrounded by water, and I knew how to take advantage of the big boom. I developed an innate ability to predict which way the shipping market was going to go. I invested heavily in secondhand ships and, soon, TMT was operating over a 100 vessels, from bulk carriers to supertankers and liquefied natural gas carriers. These ships could cost as much as nine figures and take a few years to build, whereas secondhand ships could be ready to roll in a matter of months. I believed my investment strategy would set my family up for generations to come.

Unfortunately, I was wrong.

After nine years of litigation and law suits, during which I've gained access to thousands of private, undisclosed documents from the biggest banks in the UK and US and the brokers who worked with them, there's now absolutely no doubt in my mind that TMT's accounts were hijacked during the financial crisis of 2007–2008, to provide liquidity (money) in what was one of the greatest scams in financial history. When the banks ran out of cash, I became their unlimited ATM machine, connected through confidential money routes between British and European banks and through JPMorgan Chase to US banks.

Manipulating TMT's accounts was like taking candy from a baby. The banks sussed us out and realized we were perfect for their plans. We came skipping into their yard, full of trust and eager to be accepted, with our pockets full of gold—and they mugged us! In the ten years since 2008 those same financial terrorists believe they've gotten away with the perfect crime.

This book is to tell them they have not!

In their efforts to save a corrupt and mismanaged investment industry they almost destroyed the company my father worked so hard to build and I, after him, had continued to expand. But TMT's death throe wasn't their only victim— you, the public, were also scammed in this effort to save the big banks from disaster. The global economy suffered, and is still suffering, and the population of the world is still living with the fallout, in the form of poverty and "austerity."

In this book, I'll be exploring the actions of two banks in particular—Royal Bank of Scotland, the UK's biggest bank at the time; and JPMorgan Chase, a multinational holding company with headquarters on Wall Street—and how they worked together to get as much as they could out of the US Federal Reserve by intentionally creating volatility on the commodities market. For those of you who don't know, the commodities market trades in agricultural products like wheat, coffee, cocoa, fruit, and sugar (soft commodities), and hard commodities like gold, iron ore, diamonds, and oil. It's a sensitive place and the smallest swing of the needle has huge consequences. Almost everything is affected if the commodity market becomes volatile and traders get scared, which triggers panic selling. The price of iron ore shot up, the price of steel shot up, the price of oil fluctuated wildly, and the world was days away from not just a financial crash, but a crash in every market. A crash like that would have been felt not just by the financial markets, but by everybody.

Recession turning into depression—1930s style.

Why did they do it? Because of the logic of "moral hazard." Moral hazard, in the context of this book, is a lack of responsibility, a failure to guard against recklessness because you know you're protected against the consequences of your actions. The banks knew that, if they created a crisis, they could blackmail governments into coming to their rescue as white knights to avoid a depression. Government has deep pockets and the banks saw this as a way of getting their sticky fingers into those pockets. They also found a way to enter the world of shipping, my world, through a little known financial product called Forward Freight Agreements (FFAs).

As I'll show, it takes nothing more than creating a couple of shadow accounts, a fake merger here and there, a lot of inside information, and a few big bets on future commodities. TMT was one of their biggest victims, they managed to strip a multibillion dollar company of almost all its value in under five years and get away with it—or think they did. Consequently, I consider it to be my duty to present the evidence and theories I have amassed while attempting to sue both Royal Bank of Scotland and JPMorgan Chase for their irresponsible, negligent, and, frankly, criminal behavior. It hasn't been an easy journey through the thorny tangle of policy, loan terms, legal transcripts, and censured boardroom minutes that I've spent years trawling. Long days and evenings while, around me, the vessels I spent years building and chartering floundered in shipyards, with their crews stranded in foreign countries.

Although I've now compiled enough evidence to begin to tell the tale of how the big banking establishments saw a crisis coming and profited from it at the expense of TMT and other independent businesses, there's still a larger tale to be told and I'm working on that. I intend this book to be the first of many investigative forays into the criminal conspiracy that created the most devastating recession the world has ever suffered. Each book will cover a new episode, or chapter, in the crisis, and will attempt to demystify the various tactics that politicians and financiers use to obscure their actions, from cooked-up balance sheets to stultifying terminology, from burner phones to other methods of evasion.

What happened to TMT, to my family, and to many other companies and families during the crisis was unforgivable; but if, through truthfully examining the experience, we can force the global financial elite to change their ways and become responsible contributors to society, then it might just be worth it. Change is coming, for better or for worse, and it's coming fast. Let's harness the energy of dissatisfaction and disenfranchisement and direct it towards those responsible for the inevitable self-destruction of our financial sector. There are other ways to live and behave. There are other ways to bank. The reason why every attempt to reignite our economy has failed and why real-time earnings and interest rates are still stagnant, is because no one has correctly diagnosed the problem. You can't prescribe the correct medicine unless you have the right diagnosis.

Over the course of this series of books, I intend to provide just that!

Working with my father when I was young

DEREGULATION: THE CAUSE OF A CRISIS

Let's go back a bit, to the 1980s. The Depository Institutions and Monetary Control Act of 1980 in the USA phased out restrictions on banks' financial practices and broadened their lending powers. Then, in 1982, the Garn-St. Germain Depository Institutions Act began the process of serious banking deregulation. Similarly, in 1986, the British Government deregulated the financial institutions in the City of London and opened up that "enclave" to international financial involvement and activity. Deregulation was an integral part of Reganomics in the USA and Thatcherite economic policy in the UK.

This deregulation continued into the 1990s and the new millennium. In the USA, in 1999, provisions that prohibited a bank from owning other financial institutions were repealed, removing the barrier that existed between Wall Street investment banks and depository banks (specialists in the securities investment market), providing a government stamp of approval for a universal risk-taking banking model. Investment banks like Lehman Brothers would now be in direct competition with commercial banks.

The key issue was when the IRS asked IT millionaires to pay their taxes. They suddenly started selling stock and the Dot-Com boom collapsed. This led to huge losses for investment banks such as JPMorgan, Chase Manhattan, Bear Stearns, Lehman Brothers, and many others on Wall Street. They needed another source of income. JPMorgan merged with Chase Manhattan, which was announced on September 13, 2000, without much reaction from financial commentators. When the dust settled only top-tier investment banks—such as JPMorgan Chase, Citibank, Bank of America,

Goldman Sachs, and Morgan Stanley—were left, along with three middle-tier securities firms—Merrill Lynch, Lehman Brothers, and Bear Stearns. They needed to come up with a money-making device to replace Dot-Com. That device was the (risky) sub-prime mortgage.

In 2004 the US Securities and Exchange Commission allowed investment banks to substantially increase the level of debt they were taking on, fueling the growth in mortgage-backed securities and supporting sub-prime mortgages. Financial institutions in the shadow banking system (unregulated activities by regulated institutions) were not subject to the same regulations as depository banks. Regulators and accounting standard-setters relaxed their rules, allowing balance sheets to be manipulated with complex structured investments that masked the weakness of the firm and the degree of risk being taken.

So, nobody really knew the true financial position of the major banks. The Federal Reserve in the USA kept the derivatives market unregulated and allowed the self-regulation of over-the-counter (OTC) derivatives. An OTC is a private trade that's conducted between two individual traders, as opposed to going through a regulated exchange like the London Stock Exchange. Derivatives are simply contracts that get their value from the performance of an underlying entity, like an asset or an interest rate, and they were called "financial weapons of mass destruction" as early as 2003. What all this means is that, from as early as the 1980s, the banks were increasingly not responsible to anyone but themselves.

A recipe for disaster, given the nature of greed.

The proverbial hit the fan in 2007–2008.

The financial crisis of 2008 is considered to have been the worst of its kind since the Great Depression of the 1930s. It began with a crisis in the sub-prime mortgage market in the USA. Excessive risk-taking by the banks triggered a massive bailout to prevent the collapse of the international financial system. The crisis was followed by a global economic downturn, recession, a debt crisis, and affected the lives of ordinary working people through the world—except for the bankers who caused it. They got richer.

Most of these high-risk sub-prime loans originated between 2004 and 2007, after the relaxing of credit lending standards by investment and commercial banks. Sub-prime wasn't any less risky, it was just that the banks accepted the higher risk, believing the government would bail them out if things got bad. It was a win-win situation: make money from high-risk, high-interest loans if people kept paying their mortgages; make money from the government if they did not. Even so, there weren't enough people with bad credit taking out risky loans to satisfy the investment banks' appetite for the lucrative end product. So they started making bets that were far beyond the value of the underlying mortgage, using derivatives called credit default swaps (CDSs). A fairly simple explanation is, in the corporate debt markets the buyer of a CDS pays the seller a series of fees or "spreads" in return for a payoff if the loan defaults. It's a kind of insurance against non-payment. With sub-prime, if the mortgage defaulted, the buyer received the face value of the loan and the seller took possession of the defaulted mortgage. It was like gambling for very high stakes—the buyer of the CDS was betting it would default and the seller was betting it wouldn't. CDSs were unregulated and anyone could buy them, even if they didn't own the loan in question—like betting on a horse race when you don't own a horse.

Interest rates were lowered to soften the effects of the Dot-Com collapse and the 9/11 attacks, and to combat the risk of deflation. Potential home-buyers were offered adjustable or "teaser" mortgage rates—that was to get them hooked, the teaser rate would only stay that low for a limited period of time, then it would climb until it reached the full indexed rate. The expansion of the sub-prime home mortgage sector was also encouraged by a US Federal Law (the CRA) that dropped the required FICO (US credit rating agency) score. These risky loans were then bundled to form mortgage-backed securities (MBSs), which is just an umbrella term that included CDOs and any financial product that used mortgages as an asset. CDOs are "collateralized debt obligations," loans grouped together where the loan is the collateral and declared "safe" by the credit rating agencies. This made it easier to qualify and made sub-prime lending a riskier business. Proof of income and assets were de-emphasized and low or no documentation was required. One product that gained wide popularity was the "no income, no job, no asset verification" or NINJA mortgage. These loans were called "liar loans," but nobody cared, underwriting practices that were weak at best and, at worst, fraudulent, collapsed completely. Lending banks were pressurized to falsify documents and sell mortgages to Wall Street banks, eager to make fast profits, with enormous fees accruing throughout the chain, from the mortgage brokers to the investment banks.

One underwriter said, 'If you had a pulse, we gave you a loan.'

Financial innovations allowed banks to get round such regulations as remained. Off-balance sheet securitization (hiding debt) and the "shadow banking system" (financial black market) made it difficult for regulators to monitor risk levels and impossible to reorganize in the event of bankruptcy, thus sealing the deal for eventual government bailouts. Prior to the crisis, financial institutions became highly leveraged, increasing their risky investments and reducing their liquidity. The riskiest mortgages were funded through the shadow banking system and competition from dodgy lenders pressurized more traditional institutions to lower their own underwriting standards and take on high-risk loans. Lack of transparency about risk exposures prevented markets from evaluating those risks and made the crisis far worse than it might have been otherwise.

The mortgage-backed securities could be sold as "low-risk" because they were backed by CDS insurance. Mortgage brokers could pass on these sub-primes and their associated risk in that way. High (and loose) mortgage approval rates drove up housing prices and this, along with the lower interest rates, encouraged more borrowing against the increased "equity," creating a bubble. CDOs became synthetic CDOs—that is, betting on the bets, then betting on the bets on the bets, and so on. The boom in complex financial products multiplied the number of participants connected to a mortgage—brokers, originators, securitizers, due diligence firms, agents, trading desks, investors, and insurance providers. With increasing distance from the underlying asset, these participants relied more and more on indirect information like FICO scores, creditworthiness appraisals, and risk management. This opened the way for misjudgment, fraud, and market collapse.

The new products got so complicated that regulators and rating agencies couldn't calculate the risks and relied on the banks themselves to give them the correct information. As financial assets became more complex and harder to value, investors were reassured by the regulators—accepting as valid those complex mathematical models that showed the risks were much lower than they actually were. One such indicator was Li's Gaussian Copula Formula (a mathematical equation), that linked the price of CDSs with the price of MBSs and that was used by most investors. Its limitations were never properly understood and this error of judgment allowed trillions of dollars to be swallowed up, brought the financial sector to its knees and put the survival of the global banking system in danger. High delinquency rates led to a rapid devaluation of financial products like mortgage-backed securities, derivatives, and credit default swaps. As value plummeted, buyers evaporated and banks that were heavily invested in these assets experienced a liquidity crisis.

It was, as George Soros said, 'A shocking abdication of responsibility!'

So, overvaluation of sub-prime mortgages was based on the assumption that house prices would continue to rise and all would be well as the bubble continued to expand. They didn't—they fell. Interest rates rose, borrowers defaulted, and lenders foreclosed. As well as the widespread failures in financial regulation and supervision, and the breakdown in accountability and ethics, it was a catalog of chaos—high-risk and complex financial products that few people truly understood, conflicts of interest, lack of transparency, and the excesses of Wall Street.

All driven by that underlying all-too-human trait—GREED!

When the Federal Reserve Bank of New York initiated the Primary Dealer Credit Facility (PDCF) in 2008, after the fall of the investment bank Bear Stearns in March, it allowed 17 eligible financial institutions to exchange sub-prime mortgage-backed securities for funding. They intended it as a way of pumping liquidity back into the financial sector without directly loaning or bailing anyone out. The actions and reactions of the Fed, the US Treasury, the Bank of England, the Bank for International Settlements (BIS), the European Central Bank and top tier financial corporations were varied, strange, and occasionally badly documented. As Hank Paulson, the Treasury Secretary who oversaw the Lehman Brothers bankruptcy and the American International Group (AIG) bailout said when he was on the stand for the Financial Crisis Inquiry Commission:

'I can't off-hand list all the unusual measures the Fed took.'

Unusual measures is an apt description. However, the banks saw those measures as an opportunity to make a quick profit and, using the same tactics employed by money launderers working for drug cartels, they hijacked my company, Today Makes Tomorrow, and used its accounts to fund a scheme that saw them selling securities to the NY Fed for 25 times their value. That means you, the taxpayer, purchased those securities from banks like Royal Bank of Scotland and JPMorgan Chase for 25 times their true worth.

To the ordinary man or woman in the street, it can sometimes seem that upheavals in the financial sector are remote and have nothing to do with them. The terrible truth is, people die because of a financial crisis, and that's not even counting the 10,000 suicides across Europe and North America. Children starve, others fail to reach their full potential. Pensioners lose their incomes and are forced to rely on the charity of families and food banks. More than 30 million people lost their jobs after 2008. The crazy historical high for iron ore price manipulation meant that about 150 poor nations weren't able to complete building roads, bridges and other infrastructure projects Crime increased exponentially and democracy began to fracture and turn in on itself, as we've seen across the USA and Europe. Extreme politics started to look more appealing to the average voter after they watched one group of greedy Machiavellians destroy their life savings and get away with it—not just get away with it, but profit from it! I hope that, one day, the people responsible for the financial crisis will be prosecuted for their crimes and the financial sector will become an appropriately regulated contributor to society, as opposed to the self-propagating parasite it is.

They said that sub-prime default rates over 8% (the crisis line) were "impossible." They weren't. The banks realized their toxic assets were reaching maturity and serious liquidity problems were on the horizon so, to avoid paying out and losing billions, they refused to devalue their junk bonds (CDOs and synthetic CDOs) until they could get rid of them, unloading them onto unsuspecting customers. In effect, instead of taking the hit, they decided to crash the whole system—not just the financial system, but the whole system! They brought the world to the brink of total collapse to save themselves. It sounds outlandish, doesn't it? But don't forget, we're talking about banks that have been prosecuted for rigging Libor (the benchmark lending rate), for mis-selling financial products, for money laundering, fraud, embezzlement, and front-running. We're discussing a culture of people who pride

themselves on making money, not on their morality. These
financial behemoths are so big that, when they shift their
weight, they create earthquakes.

When I started my investigations into the financial crisis
and how my company was used, I met a banker from Russia
who worked for the Dutch bank ABN AMRO during those
strange years. He told me he'd seen a whiteboard in one of
the offices all scribbled over with systematic illustrations and
complex flow-charts. Before the door was slammed in his
face, he managed to read the title, How To Save The World
Financial System. It's my belief that there would've been
similar whiteboards in every major financial institution.

Some plans exploited the PDCF, others exploited margin
calls and front-running on forward freight agreements (FFAs),
some used swap agreements (derivative contracts), while a
few banks even went so far as to intentionally bankrupt and
liquidate small businesses in their desperate hunt for liquidity.
For a while, most managed to balance on the edge between the
lawful and the unlawful. They tried to steal without becoming
thieves—the problem was, there was no new money in the
system to steal. They had to get someone to print the money
for them and, for that, they needed the Federal Reserve Bank
of America.

And they needed me!

Wall Street and the City of London

THE ANATOMY OF THE SCAM

Let's make a couple of assumptions at the start of this chapter. Firstly, the assumption that top-tier bankers are accustomed to and unfazed by the prospect of profiting from the misfortune of others. They see themselves as innovators, trapped in an eternal (but mutually beneficial) struggle against the regulations, rather than as lawbreakers. I've heard bankers, who have walked a very thin tight-rope between cunning and fraud, explain that it's good when they find a new loophole and exploit it—because it teaches the regulators to come up with better regulations. Computer hackers who break into government websites often cite a similar excuse. I think this is an especially lax moral argument, since it ignores the individuals and businesses the regulations are meant to protect.

To give you one example of banks profiting from misfortune, I remember clearly how the Western banks swept into Japan and Asia during the infamous recession that was caused by the collusion between the Yakuza (crime syndicate) and Japanese "zombie banks" (with no net worth). They bought up property and land at bargain-basement prices while the austerity measures suggested by the US Treasury suffocated businesses. For them, the leveling of another nation's economy was nothing more than an opportunity to get a stronger presence on the international financial stage. If there's a new way to make a profit, whether it's in an oil-rich but politically unstable state, or an obscure and mathematically complex way of turning personal mortgages into gambling chips, they'll do it. In the short term, this may benefit their domestic economies by creating booms in sectors that supersede their usual pace of growth. However, this growth is stimulated and functions much like caffeine in the human anatomy, in that the high will always be followed by a crash. The only people who always profit from these boom and bust cycles are the banks that are clever enough to get out before their Frankenstein creations begin to implode.

Considering the Libor scandal, the mis-selling of PPIs, HSBC and Standard Chartered Bank's collusion with money launderers, the rigging of the foreign exchange and currency markets, to name but a few of the banking misdemeanours in recent years, I'd be surprised if many readers would disagree with my first assumption. It might, however, surprise you to learn that this trait isn't restricted to banks, but extends to the regulatory bodies that are supposed to police them. For example, the man who led the charge of the Western banks during the Asian crisis was the same man America turned to for help in the financial crisis of 2008, Timothy Geithner.

Timothy Geithner was president of the Federal Reserve of New York in 2008, the most powerful of the 12 Fed districts, until he replaced Hank Paulson as US Treasurer after Barack Obama was inaugurated as the 44th President. He was the person in a central position of power during the build-up to the crisis and its aftermath. By the time he was appointed to the Fed, he'd already been working for the Treasury for over 20 years—he was working for them in Tokyo when the Asian crisis hit. Officially he was there to help the troubled nations recover, but it didn't always seem that way. When the Japanese Finance Ministry attempted to create an Asian Monetary Fund so that the affected countries could collaborate in the recovery and prevention of another crash, Geithner made sure it never got off the ground. Why? So the IMF could enforce an austerity policy and cut spending. Asian companies had to pay back loans, became distressed, and could be bought out cheaply. In Leo Panitch's article in *The Guardian*, he states

> *Geithner orchestrated the opposition to this [AMF] by other Asian states (including China), thereby ensuring that*

the Treasury was able to deny 'any charge that the imperial Americans were blocking an Asian solution'.

From this I think it's clear that Geithner wasn't only an economist and civil servant, but also a politician, with a politician's aptitude for manipulation. He was one of the first Federal Reserve presidents to welcome the "expertise" of Wall Street bankers into the Fed. It provoked controversy and conflicts of interest regarding neutrality and a "revolving door" system of secret maneuvring.

In his memoir, *Stress Test*, Geithner comes across as unapologetic, sometimes sulky, and more than a little sensitive to the criticisms that have hounded him since the crisis—that he lied and didn't accept accountability for printing the money that saved Wall Street. Because he's seen, rightly or wrongly, as a man of Wall Street, who thought only of preserving and maintaining the profits of the non-traditional banking sector. He believed it was better to make billions from risky trades than to play it safe and generate less revenue for the economy. This would seem to indicate that he was more interested in how to contain a crisis than how to prevent one. The only problem was, he'd have to wait for a crisis to hit before he could test his theories. He wouldn't have to wait long.

The last part of his book is interesting—he cited that he didn't send or take any emails, or make any notes during his reign. So, he wrote from memory?

The financial crisis began to smolder in Europe during August 2007, migrated to the USA in March 2008 and came to a climax in September 2008. But none of it went how Geithner imagined it would. This wasn't a downturn that could be easily managed by lowering inflation rates and stimulating the economy with a few industry handouts—it was an unstoppable forest fire. The panicked, sleep-deprived, and, at times, incoherently inconsistent way the Federal Reserve attempted to provide liquidity wasn't difficult for the banks to exploit. Most of us have heard of TARP (Troubled Asset Relief Program), some might have even heard of the

PDCF as well, but who knows how the CPFF (Commercial Paper Funding Facility) works, or the TSLF (Term Securities Lending Facility), or currency swaps and central bank lines? Each and every one of these lending facilities were set up by the Fed from scratch, mostly in under two days, and had the capacity to be exploited by the bankers who knew how to rig the system in their favor, and had the motivation to do so.

All around the globe, steady giants like AIG, Bear Sterns, Morgan Stanley, Royal Bank of Scotland, General Electric and General Motors were crumbling and taking hundreds of thousands of jobs with them. The neutered regulatory bodies had passively allowed the outlandishly dangerous sub-prime bubble to expand in the first place, so now they were hardly in a position to make sure no one was taking unfair advantage of the myriad ways to access credit suddenly appearing all over the place. Not only did the bankers have the motive and the skills to exploit these new credit-providing schemes, but they also had the opportunity.

The second assumption we're going to make is that top-tier financiers, hypothetically, could provoke a short-term and controllable crisis in the Western financial system. Why would they do that? Well, they might have wanted to force the hand of the Federal Reserve and other centralized banks, and then profit from a compromised and panicked response from those banks. This, of course, may be harder to prove than the first assumption, but it's what I intend to do in this chapter. I'll show you how, with the right motivation, a group of CEOs and industry insiders could have intentionally created a global recession between 2004 and 2009. My investigations have led me to believe that four banks were at the heart of this "scam"—JPMorgan Chase, Royal Bank of Scotland and, to a lesser degree, Goldman Sachs and Barclays. Other corporations, like the Anglo-Australian mining firms of BHP Billiton and Rio Tinto, and heavyweight shipping industry honchos like Clarksons, ICAP (Intercapital plc), and GFI were also implicated. I'll go into more detail about each of these companies and the parts they played later, but first I would like, before I get into the mechanics of their actions, to air the caveat that every person involved probably thought they were doing the right thing.

To this day bankers at JPMorgan Chase herald their CEO, Jamie Dimon—a self-made billionaire—as the "man who saved the world." Barack Obama—who believed that JPMorgan Chase was one of the best managed banks in the USA—himself said, 'Jamie Dimon shouldn't be punished for doing a pretty good job managing an enormous portfolio.'

Dimon has a vast fan base in the financial sector and has, since the crash, been appointed by Donald Trump to give advice on the economy. He's a hugely influential man and regarded as a strong, outspoken opponent of increased financial regulation and is, reportedly, a capitalist with a moral backbone, reminiscent of the great Victorian industrialists, deeply concerned with his civic duty. This civic duty has found itself, from time to time, at odds with his other prevailing belief, that the market knows best. He was probably caught between two solutions in 2008, and the years leading up to it: alerting the authorities to the building downturn by opening up JPMorgan's books completely and transparently; or trying to fix it himself with a team of Wall Street reservoir dogs. I can see why he chose the latter. No one likes bad press less than Jamie Dimon and the latter option was the only hope he had to preserve his stellar reputation.

The factors that turned an economic downturn into a crippling credit crunch were primarily, without doubt, the fault of the unregulated financial industry—but many would argue that, without the active response of its leaders, the fallout might have been much worse. So, yes, laws were broken, but I'm not overlooking the fact that, without these illegal "solutions," the world could be suffering much more than it is today. And the entrepreneur in me can't help but admire the cunning and skill it took to pull it all off. The illegality of the scam doesn't interest me as much as the premise that the cover-up has prevented us from seeing what went wrong in the first place. And, while it's alright to admire the innovation that stopped a worse crisis, it's rather ironic to know that the same kind of innovation started it.

With the Head of Clarkson research in 2007

With the Chairman of the Baltic Exchange in 2008

THE RACE TO SAVE THE BANKS

The race to save the banks began back in 2007. Goldman Sachs had already started shorting the sub-prime mortgage bubble. Shorting stock is, as Michael Lewis pinioned so effectively in his book-turned-movie, The Big Short, a way of betting against the market. If you think a company is going to do well, then you buy "long" stocks, but if you think it's going to fail, then you can "short" it. It's a complicated way of dealing shares that not only predicts failure, but can also contribute towards it if enough people start shorting that company. Think of it like this: buying CDSs is shorting CDOs; you're betting the CDO will default, so you buy a CDS as insurance. Get it? If Goldman Sachs was shorting the sub-prime bubble as early as 2004, it means they knew a crash was coming and they were planning on making as much money as they could.

The world of high finance is small. Most of the top players visit the same half-dozen golf clubs, restaurants, resorts, bars, and conferences. Almost all of them would be sending their children to one of the top 20 private schools in the world. What I'm trying to say is, in a gated enclave like that, secrets are difficult to keep. If Goldman Sachs were shoring the market in 2004, then you can bet your life that the other three—JPMorgan Chase, Royal Bank of Scotland, and Barclays—knew all about it.

Even if they didn't believe the storm was coming, they would've certainly started checking the weather report. One way to do this would be to recruit experts in the field—and that's exactly what they did. A couple of years ago I ran into Angus Paul at one of the functions set up for members of the shipping industry to mingle and network. Angus Paul was, until 2016, head of coal freight at Glencore, which meant he was chartering ships for one of the largest and most influential mining companies in the world. He was also in charge of a great deal of commodity trading. If Glencore wanted to sell futures on their coal, thus reducing the risk that coal prices would drop down the line and cause a loss, then Angus Paul was the man to do it. Glencore is tenth on the Fortune Global 500 list and the leading marketer of commodities. Commodities is financial-speak for any resource worth fighting over: oil, coal, zinc, copper, grain and other primary agricultural products, natural gas, iron, diamonds, and so on. Glencore has mines and outposts all over the world and has a patchy history when it comes to corporate responsibility. In 2012 the Democratic Republic of the Congo accused them of employing children as young as ten, after undercover investigators discovered the kids digging copper and cobalt in "hand-dug mineshafts 150 feet deep, without safety or breathing equipment." Glencore denied the accusation and, as so often happens, the news moved on and the allegations gently faded away without any resolutions being made.

Angus Paul, like many of the shipping industry's inner circle, wasn't as happy to speak to me as he would have been in 2006, but that's only to be expected. Back then I was a billionaire making trades so huge that the market shifted in my wake—now I was an eccentric outsider. Actually, I never realized how freeing that would be. When I was a billionaire it was difficult to get the real truth from people because they would invariably be trying to get something from me, whether they realized it or not, and would say what they thought I wanted to hear. I occasionally felt, when I entered a room, like a headmaster walking into a class full of chattering teenagers. When they saw me, the laughter fell away and everyone assumed their best behavior, not wanting to fall out of favor. Now they don't care and they'll tell me anything. I've learned far more about human behavior after my fall from grace than I ever dreamed possible.

I asked Angus Paul what was happening at Glencore in the years leading up to the crisis and, since I no longer mattered that much to him, he gave me a long look and told me that, in those days, one of his main concerns was managing the new interest shown by the banks in the physical commodity markets, especially shipping. He told me British and US bankers were continuously visiting Ivan Glassenberg, the CEO of Glencore, in Zug, Switzerland. Zug is a beautiful town surrounded by mountains and lakes, that has become a center of international trade thanks to its enticingly low taxes. Angus Paul told me they came to Zug to find out how the physical commodity market might work in conjunction with financial derivatives such as FFAs. They already knew they could make huge bets on insurance and debt, but would the same system work if they were to use, say, oil futures instead? The answer was yes and, in 2007, the banks started to trade heavily in future derivatives on the commodity market.

There's a definition of future derivatives in the Glossary at the beginning of this book, but I'm going to take a moment to explain what I mean by the term, before I go into the details of how it was possible for a group of bankers to create a false sense of volatility on the commodity market. As I've said, there are all kinds of futures—coal, iron, wheat—and, particular to this book, there are futures in ships. Let's imagine for a moment I have a tonne of coal and I'm worried that prices are going to fall. I want to sell my coal now, at its current price, but nobody wants it yet. There's no demand. What do I do? If I have to wait until someone needs the coal, its price may have fallen. This is a problem that's plagued miners and farmers for thousands of years, but the solution is quite simple. I find a buyer who'll need the coal in, say, six months time, but he's worried the price will rise. He doesn't want to wait six months and get ripped off, so we make a deal—he promises he'll buy my coal in six months time, at its current price. So, he's purchased a "future"—a contract that states he'll own my coal in six months time. You'll already have guessed that a future is a two-sided bet—if the price goes up, he wins; if it goes down, I win.

But then middlemen start getting involved, who might not want a tonne of coal dumped on their front lawn. No, these traders hope to sell on the future, long before the delivery is due to be made. They just want to buy low and sell high, like they're already doing on the stock market, and they make the same bet as me and my original coal buyer. Futures in shipping are called forward freight agreements (FFAs, which I've already mentioned) and this might sound strange at first but, when you think about it, it makes sense. If someone needs to ship quinoa from Ecuador to England in time for your summer salads, they might well want to book a ship in advance, in case prices rise. If you book an airline flight in advance, you'll probably get a better price than if you book on the day—on the other hand, if you book a hotel room at the last minute, you might get a better price if the hotel still has rooms vacant, than you would if you booked in advance. It's just matter of knowing the market and being prepared to take a risk. In trading, as soon as someone's selling a future, there'll be a trader trying to jump on it to make a quick buck. I've traded heavily in FFAs myself, since it was a quick, albeit risky, way to generate profits, which I could then pour back into chartering and repairing my tankers.

My query is this: what if the bankers' sudden interest in the commodity market and shipping wasn't just the natural magnetism that draws a banker towards a new money-making scheme? What if this interest in the commodity market was sparked by a group of highly intelligent industry leaders who realized that, if they were going to solve their own crisis, they would have to create a problem so vast that governments would have to step in.

Think about it!

At the time of the financial crisis, Hank Paulson was the US Treasury Secretary and he'd said, on many occasions, that he firmly believed in a laissez-faire approach to the markets.

He believed in capitalism. He believed that, if you allowed free trade to go its own way, then the survivors would naturally accrue wealth and the losers would disappear without ever troubling the wider economy. Capitalism, in Paulson's view, was essentially "red in tooth and claw," just like Tennyson considered nature itself to be in his prophetically titled poem, In Memoriam. Paulson's most repeated quote was,

'An open, competitive and liberalized financial market can effectively allocate scarce resources in a manner that promotes stability and prosperity far better than governmental intervention.'

Hank Paulson wasn't the man you'd go to for a bailout. He was, ideologically, the opposite of that man.

But the banks were running out of money and, after all, Hank Paulson was one of them at the end of the day. He'd been the CEO of Goldman Sachs before Bush asked him to be Treasury Secretary and many still thought of him as their inside man in Washington. They knew their CDOs and synthetic CDOs were bad; they knew it wouldn't be long before enough reached maturity to let the proverbial cat out of the bag. And they knew, when that happened they'd be in serious trouble. If they were going to save their jobs, they'd need the kind of cash injection only the government could provide. The question was, how on earth were they going to convince a man like Hank Paulson to betray the economic theory he held most dear? How would they get him to abandon the "all's fair in love and trade" approach, in favor of quantitative easing?

The US Treasury in Washington DC

SHIPPING

There were rumors circulating in 2007 that bankers, desperate to start trading in FFAs and future derivatives, asked brokers to place microphones on world-renowned trading floors, so they could find out exactly who was doing that trading already and how much they were willing to spend. If these rumors were true, then it wouldn't take long for the banks to build up a highly accurate picture of who ruled the waves. Of course, rumors like that are often spread about new competitors, so I'll leave it up to the readers to make up their own minds. What we do know is that the banks, in a short space of time, wooed their way into working with the world's largest shipping brokers, like Clarksons, ICAP, SSY and GFI. They did this by shifting trades from the traditional OTC market to the London Clearing House (LCH).

The following section of this book is very complicated, so I'll try to spell it out as clearly as possible, without it becoming too long-winded. Hopefully.

Let's take another pause to explain in more detail what the OTC market is and how it differs from the LCH. As a trading device over-the-counter pretty much does what it says on the tin—much like how I could walk up to any stall in a market and exchange money for a bag of apples. In OTC trading I can approach any other counterparty and work out an arrangement without any middleman or fixed pricing (fixed interest rate swap) to make a deal. It's simple, quick, and relies on a great deal of mutual trust. On the market, the stallholder is trusting that my money isn't counterfeit and I'm trusting that the apples he's put in the bag aren't bad. Because OTC markets are unregulated and quite secretive, whichever side of the trade has the most market information, also has the greatest advantage. If the stallholder knows there's someone selling apples cheaper than him down the market, he's not going to tell me. As a seller, he wants to get as high a price as possible, even if that means profiting from the buyer's ignorance. Equally, as the buyer, if I know that his apples are of such good quality they could easily fetch a higher price, I'm not going to tell him.

The big problem with the OTC markets was, there were few safety nets and, if a trade deal went wrong, counterparties would be left horribly exposed (unprotected from loss) if the other counterparties couldn't pay. It's one of the abiding rules of the financial markets that all risk will eventually be purchased and packaged (cleaned up). The people who eventually found a way to minimize the brokers' risk were Rolfe & Nolan, who wrote the margin call software that makes the London Clearing House function. In the LCH, the banks promise to guarantee the brokers' exposure and ensure consistent and timely payments, thereby solving two major problems with OTC trades. However, in order to trade with the LCH, you have to be represented by a major clearing bank that is a member of the LCH. Which meant that many shipping magnates, myself included, who traditionally banked with financial institutions from their own countries, now had to move to the powerful international banks. What these banks had to offer the OTC trader was the promise of security in an infamously volatile sector of the commodity market.

By the second half of 2007, they started to approach the big shipping companies one by one, through shipbrokers like Clarksons, ICAP, SSY, GFI or other major FFA brokers, and helped them to start trading with the LCH. These shipping companies were like cat-nip to the banks – they were the ideal clients to have at a time when they were desperate to increase their cash reserves – privately owned, inordinately wealthy and interested in trading. Royal Bank of Scotland in particular, who had a long established relationship with a powerful cohort of Greek shipping families, began pursuing other maritime firms with steely resolve. Furthermore, RBS already had London Clearing House trade with Oldendorf Carriers, the largest shipping company in Germany, which had an equivalent trading volume as my company, Today Makes Tomorrow. So what, you might say? What does that mean? Well, it means RBS was front-running together with Oldendorf. Look at it like this; TMT buys, RBS sells, then Oldendorf buys. TMT sells, RBS buys, then Oldendorf sells. TMT and Oldendorf were trading the same amount on the same day and that's no coincidence. Over eighteen months, TMT and Oldendorf consistently made the same trades. This is evidence of criminal front running. The RBS trader used TMT money to create the derivatives targeted to be used in the future. There were two separate Oldendorf accounts there is evidence and analysis of the facts, to conclude this narrative.

Strangely, the TMT account officer for FFA shipping derivatives was supposed to be Russell Goodwin, but it was CDO/CDS expert Gerard Joynson who took it over. He had no knowledge of FFAs because TMT had never traded with RBS Shipping before, nor with prop trader Doug Guernsey. Basically, TMT's FFA account was faked—it was created on US dollar savings account number 09878 and just described as "TMT FFA—Clearing." An independent accountancy firm has since commented: "The account application forms had a number of irregularities and abnormalities and appear to have been casually prepared." With regard to the way the account was being managed by RBS, the accountancy firm had this to say:

> *Various irregularities were identified from the daily statements, such as inconsistent preparation, substantial typographic errors, unreconciled balances and arithmetic errors, large quantities of trade cancellations, incomplete monthly statements, unknown items on the daily statements and unusual practices for margin calls.*

RBS, JPMorgan Chase, Barclays, Goldman Sachs, and Morgan Stanley now had major stakes and influence in the commodity markets—especially Goldman Sachs and Morgan

Stanley, who already owned physical shipping businesses under various subsidiaries. The problem to come was, those major banks didn't have the infrastructure in place to handle clients who were used to making huge and complex trades every single day and who now, to avail themselves of the security the LCH promised, required the banks to calculate and regulate margin calls (demands for cash) and asset evaluations swiftly and accurately. Unsurprisingly, they were so desperate to reel in big clients and a fresh source of liquidity, they were prepared to promise that they could implement the quality of service needed.

A special team was formed in the futures division of RBS Singapore, which had no idea about FFAs, to handle my company, TMT. They were supervised by James Travis and Neena Birdee, who were spies from London, sent out to monitor the Asia division and focus on TMT, and also Rio Tinto in Singapore and Melbourne.

The sudden structural shift from OTC trades to the LCH was mainly an issue of settlement (payment) methods. FFAs now had two settlement options: LCH sudden-death margin calls (demands for money); and OTC monthly payments. The margin calls were made first by the traders, who would then receive monthly settlements from the banks if their trades were successful. The problem with this was, sudden-death margin calls were big lump sums, whereas monthly settlements were smaller amounts, so the shipping companies found themselves with less available liquidity than they were used to. In addition, brokers could now make trades that were far more complex than the traditional two-party OTC deals, and so they pushed their clients to take more and more risks, which led to several shipping companies going bust (Sanko Line in Japan, Transfield in China, and others in the USA, Ukraine, and Australia). The market sped up, the bets got bigger, and the stakes got higher, just as the global economy was starting to wobble.

The timing couldn't have been worse!

Most brick-and-mortar conservative shipping companies had no idea how to calculate margins. They said the system was safer for clients, but because most of them had only one bank clearing their trades, they paid whatever that bank asked, without really querying the calculations. The margin calculations (amount needed to bring an account up to the minimum agreed maintenance margin) were made by the banks using data compiled by Rolfe & Nolan, even though the London Stock Exchange owned half of the LCH and could easily have supplied its own data.

Rolfe & Nolan is a company owned by two hedge funds that are, in turn, connected to RBS. Whether this had an impact on the complications and miscalculations to come, I can't say; but it's another example of how incestuously entangled the banks became with the shipping industry and the commodity market. It also goes some way to explain why calculations for margin calls were being made from London, even though Wall Street, in that sense, was regarded as the financial center of the world. In my eyes it was a kind of hark back to when the British Empire ruled half the world from London, with its fleet of ships and its East India Trading Company (the first corporation to rule foreign territories with private armies and puppet administrations)—a role model for international corporations today.

At the time we all thought this was an exciting and innovative development that would bring positive changes to the FFA market and allow shipping companies to hedge (take an offsetting position to reduce risk) as much of their risk as possible. We believed it would reduce volatility, but instead it opened up our market to far more traders, brokers, middlemen, bankers, and hedge funds than it previously contained. I first realized the danger around Christmas 2007, at a party in Milan. At the time I was working, off and on, with a trader called Mattia Besozzi, who worked with ICAP, one of the largest shipping brokers in the world—Mattia became their top trader with my help. He was aggressive, smart, and knew exactly who to charm. He approached me at the party and I immediately noticed that something wasn't quite right. He looked agitated and wide-eyed, and a little paranoid, as if he felt he shouldn't be speaking to me but couldn't help himself. I listened patiently while he told me that, earlier in the day, two Wall Street hedge fund honchos with connections to Rolfe & Nolan had come to him and tried to get him to tell them about my trades and standing FFAs. (I didn't ask him whether he'd have told me about this if the amount of cocaine he'd taken hadn't loosened his tongue). It's highly illegal for hedge funds to bully details about market positions from brokers, because it leads to insider trading, front-running, market-rigging, and fraud. When he refused to divulge the information they wanted, they made a threat that chilled me to my bones when he told me.

'If we can destroy China, we can destroy you!'

It put me off the party for the rest of the night.

The threat to destroy China may or may not make much sense to you—what did China have to do with it? Well, at the time China was a major buyer of commodities like steel, iron ore, and shipping charters, as it was building up its infrastructure, cities, factories, and also preparing for the 2008 Olympics. Margin calculations, and therefore the price of chartering tankers and bulk carriers, depend on volatility in the commodities market. If volatility is raised, it raises the margin requirements and takes money out of shipping and puts it into the banks. The more volatile the market is, the higher the cost. Hedge funds and various traders now had the capability, or pretended they did, to spike volatility so much that it would become incredibly difficult and expensive for China to expand its economy in the way it had been planning. There was an intensely Western-centric outlook in the global shipping industry that only worsened once FFA trades were moved to the LCH, and all the data to determine margins was compiled with London-based software.

There were other inconsistencies which puzzled me. For instance, Mattia (the trader who was threatened by the hedge fund honchos) was allowed, by ICAP, to open a one-man office in Monaco, while Dorian Benson, the head of the GFI FFA operation, was based in Cape Town. Both, coincidentally, were in the same time zone as the London head office. This is a fairly obvious tax avoidance scheme and a way of dodging the attention of British financial regulators, since it's highly unlikely that this "one-man office" was ever occupied. Because the time zones were the same, Mattia could run the business just as well from either of the locations. An ICAP insider told me that there was one account attached to the one-man office that never lost in the LCH. As we'll later see with Bernie Madoff, an account that never loses money, that always wins on its bets, is the ultimate sign of fraud. I suspect Mattia was using the Monaco base to front-run Today Makes Tomorrow's FFAs.

Do I have evidence of Mattia's front-running? Well, there was an investigation within ICAP and they immediately changed their name from ICAP Shipbrokers to ICAP Shipping in the middle of Q3 2008, which was very odd. There was a person working with Mattia within ICAP whose job was to timestamp trades, which he delayed until the end of the day. That way Mattia could front-run with Demitris Polemis, who was a trader for Petros Pappas, the shipping magnate, who, as we'll see, was heavily involved in the plot to bankrupt TMT. ICAP's internal compliance found that the account never lost, so the two traders were fired from ICAP—without being reported to the Securities and Exchange Commission (SEC). The same kind of thing was done by a Clarkson trader called Vesalius Kallikaks—he asked me to give him details of my trades, which I refused to do.

He said, 'You know, my good friend Polys Haji-Ioannou does it and I always make money for him.'

He "made money" for other Greek clients as well, because Vesalius' job was to take care of the Greek ship owners within Clarksons.

This fraud may or may not be connected to the larger picture. Sometimes I wonder if RBS noticed Mattia's front-running scheme and our failure to report it, and this encouraged them to think that TMT would be the perfect patsy for their scam—we'll have to wait and see. But I do find it a great coincidence that Michael Spencer, the CEO of ICAP and Mattia's boss, was also the Treasurer of the Conservative Party in Britain during the financial crisis and donated £4.5 million to the Tories during the Libor scandal. This is clearly a man who knows what he wants and who to get it from. Furthermore, during Michael Spencer's time as Treasurer of the Conservative Party, the FSA regulations for keeping telephone records were shortened from five years to six months. So, British traders' phone records could be destroyed after a very short time, which seems very suspicious. What a convenient coincidence, or was it planning ahead to enable the bankers to delete their phone records and SMSs (short messenger service). Would it be crazy to wonder if he was colluding with RBS? He did found ICAP, which specializes in electronic markets. In his youth he had been a trader before being fired for misconduct. ICAP was involved in the Libor scandal, so can we assume he felt comfortable breaking banking regulations?

If there was a moment that made Fred Goodwin and his team at RBS notice me, then I think it's likely that ICAP was behind it. Which reminds me of the strange meetings I had at RBS headquarters in May and June 2008. The man I met had two objectives: 1) had I discovered how RBS were manipulating my TMT account to get funding from the New York Federal Reserve? (I hadn't); 2) did I know that TMT money was being paid into an account with a Treasury Cash Management (TCM) code and, consequently, becoming RBS' own capital? (I didn't). Call me naïve, I should've been more aware of what was happening, but I trusted Royal Bank of Scotland and that's what Fred Goodwin wanted me to do, especially while he was in negotiations for his £12 billion rights issue. Once we had those meetings, he knew I didn't have a clue what was going on and he could continue.

So, after the second meeting, RBS Shipping used shipping lawyers to find TMT's weaknesses—Hill Dickinson, Seward Kissel, and Ince & Co. Then they colluded with Petros Pappas to initiate a Rule B Attachment and increase margin calls. All this was designed to bankrupt TMT by the end of June 2008, so Plan B for the rescue of the banks could be implemented if required. At the same time, Jamie Dimon was in the process of taking over the Bernie Madoff account in New York. Dimon was good friends with Greek shipping magnates and bankers—famous people like Onassis, Angelopoulos, and others had many listed companies in New York—Zavos was a Harvard alumnus and related to George Soros. You can see how it all starts to tie together.

With the role of the LCH growing and further collusion between major shipping brokers and banks, the shipping market was growing more volatile and more sensitive almost by the day. I was beginning to wonder how much more it could take. After all, by the winter of 2007: BNP Paribas (a leading French bank) had already announced a complete evaporation of liquidity; UBS AG (a leading Swiss bank) suffered a $3.4 billion loss; most of the major banks had suffered huge mark downs at the hands of their respective regulators; and the Bank of England, famous for its reserved and cautious decisions, had sharply cut its own interest rates. My greatest fear at that time was that something would happen to directly affect the pricing and passage of ships, be it an international skirmish, the closure of a major mine, or the spiking of fuel prices. We could just about withstand the fraught financial institutions, as embroiled as we were, but could we take a direct hit?

I doubted it!

Little did I know that I and my TMT company were being manipulated to cause chaos on the commodities market so that the destabilization of the financial system could continue and the banks could come out of the mire and into millions.

Top: Blusky, the first ice class, liquified natural gas ship in the world. Designed by Nobu Sue; Centre: A Whale skimming oil in the Gulf of Mexico; Bottom: A Ladybug

MINING

I was right to be worried. At the end of December, not long after Mattia had passed on the hedge funders' harrowing threat, BHP Billiton and Rio Tinto announced a conditional merger. It was the beginning of a long and tumultuous year. BHP Billiton and Rio Tinto are both mining companies at the very heart of the commodities market. They are to metals, ores and petroleum (and therefore to the construction industry and many others) what Unilever is to food. Since they sell what we carry, their prices greatly affect the price of shipping charters and, therefore, of forward freight agreements.

I already touched on the incestuous nature of high finance—BHP Billiton had ties to Royal Bank of Scotland and Rolfe & Nolan. The Chairman of BHP Billiton was a man called Don Argus, who was once the boss of Fred "The Shred" Goodwin (the infamous CEO of RBS during the crisis) when they both worked at the Australian National Bank in 1999, around the time that BHP and Billiton originally merged. At that time, the founder of BHP was also a former chairman of the Australian National Bank and he tried to convince Fred Goodwin to become his successor. Goodwin, perhaps unfortunately, considering his catastrophic actions at RBS, declined and the job went instead to John McFarlane, who later became a colleague of his at RBS. Argus and Goodwin were close. In fact, they were more than close—they respected and looked out for each other and, when there was a chance to work together, they took it.

So, in my opinion, Don Argus and Marius Kloppers of BHP Billiton were connected in one way or another in the plot to swindle TMT and were in league with Fred Goodwin at RBS and Jamie Dimon at JPMorgan Chase.

The news of the conditional merger between the two mining companies sent shock waves through the shipping industry and the London Clearing House because the merged company would control 50% of all iron ore cargo to China. To make matters worse, only two months later Vale (a Brazilian mining company) managed to get German, Japanese and Korean steel producers to accept a 65% increase in their iron ore price. They were the first mining company to raise their price like that and, as industry tradition goes, the other mining companies were expected to follow suit and demand similar price rises. However, BHP Billiton and Rio Tinto refused to join the queue. Instead, they waited and negotiated an even higher price increase than 65%.

Stocks of iron ore had risen to a record high. If there's a lot of commodity at a port, it means it's being held up, usually because there isn't demand. If there isn't demand, consumers won't be ordering any more until they've used up what they've got and, even when they've used up that stock, they won't be re-ordering in the same quantities. So, when iron ore stocks are high at any given port, it usually means that demand has reached its peak and prices are about to fall—heavily. Ports, once they find themselves on the brink of completely filling their storage capacity, begin turning away everything except the highest-grade iron ore—with many shipments being part of long-term contracts and others part of those complex future derivatives organized by traders who still hoped to find buyers. However, as I've mentioned, three of the biggest mining companies had just negotiated huge increases in iron ore prices.

In Spring 2008 the situation got so bad that there were ships waiting outside Japanese ports because those ports simply didn't have the capacity to receive any more, as they were already taking the overflow from China. Understandably, China wasn't happy to keep paying high prices after demand for iron ore had so obviously slowed, and long drawn-out and often hostile negotiations over price began with BHP Billiton and others which, eventually, China lost. China still ended up paying astronomical prices for iron ore even though demand had subsided so greatly that the price seemed not only illogical, but also counter-intuitive for the mining companies themselves. After all, isn't it a basic precept of economics that the simplest way to increase demand is to lower the price of supply?

During this period of bargaining and uncertainty, BHP Billiton and Rio Tinto cancelled many shipments of iron ore to China, until a price was agreed and the market crashed by a whopping 30%. When the ships finally arrived, they were kept waiting outside congested Japanese ports and, as 15% of shareholders in BHP Billiton were Japanese trading companies, there were a strange number of capsizes and also a collision between two ships in the Japanese port of Kashima during the passage of a typhoon. Kashima is a port near Tokyo and it has a very small anchorage with strong winds and currents. It's interesting that these two ships hit each other and sank when the typhoon came, when many Capesize ships were there, even closer to each other. Why those two ships? Were they scuppered? All I'm saying is, questions were thrown up, but never answered.

Because of the reduction in ships, these capsizes pushed the daily spot rate (price) of the shipping market from $120,000 to $300,000. Industry rumours suspected that BHP Billiton and Rio Tinto intentionally exploited the congestion and deliberately capsized ships to inflate the freight rate. Market manipulation and the intentional creation of volatility on the commodities market—initiated by companies that were all connected, in one way or another, to Royal Bank of Scotland! As I've mentioned already, essential to the banks' plan to get as much money as possible from the Federal Reserve.

On a more personal level, all the time RBS were exploiting TMT's account and using TMT's money as if it was the bank's own.

In mid-April 2008 Gerard Joynson finally showed up, demanding $58 million because RBS forgot to charge a margin for earlier trades. It seems Clarksons intended to make a two-digit difference in the margin input, but RBS didn't explain why and had already deducted the $58 million. This began the nightmare of my disputes with Royal Bank of Scotland. Gerard Joynson took over TMT's FFA trading and, basically, took profit positions and enlarged losses. The manipulation continued and I found this analysis by the highly intelligent lawyer, Ms Deirdre Brown, about RBS' internal manipulation of my company's account to be particularly telling:

> *James Travis emails his team at RBS announcing the commodity risk charge of US$58m which he cannot reconcile. He says he cannot make the margin call as he has not received a breakdown or explanation as to how/why it was charged from LCH. He notes this has occurred on another client's account as well and asks for confirmation that no one has amended the underlying IM rate or calculation method. JT indicates concern that RBS could lose TMT as a client as a result of this discrepancy. Peter Teleki (RBS) states he has studied the PREPRI report for 16 April and it appears TMT has not been paying IM on short options. He raises the possibility that the numbers are wrong and suggests a comparison against LCH call. Email from Nigel Tan (Rolfe & Nolan—margin calculating services) to Anthony Ferris (RBS) suggests there is an issue with SPAN parameter reports which Rolfe & Nolan use to create reports sent to RBS. When Joseph Hesse (RBS) emails Peter Teleki, asking if the mismatch was due to "static of LCH not providing SPAN parameters so R&N was not generating IM on options", PT replies that he is unsure.*

> *'It's a bit strange why this has just started working.'*

> *Email from Joseph Hesse to Michael McCarthy (RBS), who is in RBS Chicago, USA, explains that the mismatch*

was due to LCH not sending settlement prices or SPAN parameters.

'The problem is threefold. LCH is bad, R&N is bad, and we need better product knowledge.'

Email from Joseph Hesse to Mick Hill and others states that the comparison between LCH calls and R&N reports proves TMT was under-margined and this probably applies to all Freight accounts. He suggests RBS needs a specialised Freight team. Email from Joseph Hesse to Gerard Joynson stating RBS needs to determine "whether R&N were getting bad info from the LCH or if R&N were just miscalculating". Email from Andrew Bentley to James Travis reporting that LCH had not sent closing prices to 17th April 2008, hence the change in TMT's account. He queries why the issue was referred to London (i.e to Gerard Joynson).

It's highly possible that instructions were coming from Fred Goodwin, pressing some people to cause confusion and to send details to Gerard Joynson.

Here I'd like to remind you again of the important call to me from FFA broker Mattia Besozzi, from his personal office, after he'd already left ICAP.

'I had a phone call from a BHPB trader and they want to do as much OTC or LCH business with TMT as you like,'

'Really?'

'Yes.

I was impressed. I'd only had two trades with BHP Billiton in the whole of the past year. Thereafter, I started to trade regularly with them.

Then, on March 15, 2008, BHP Billiton stopped trading OTC. I asked them why and they said they could no longer trade with TMT. That meant we suddenly had a significant problem in OTC trades with BHPB. It was a set-up.

I attended a meeting with BHPB in The Hague on July 20, 2008. It was another strange encounter, similar to the meetings I had had at RBS. I believed I was going there to discuss business with Mike P Henry and other BHP Billiton executives. I was kept waiting for fifty minutes and, when they finally showed up, we went for dinner to a restaurant near the center of the city. These people were from the world's largest mining company's trading division, which controls iron ore and coal shipments throughout the world, yet none of them seemed to want to talk business, they were there to see how much I knew about the manipulation of the commodities market. I knew nothing of a Deed of Termination signed on July 1 by BHP Billiton and sent to Ince & Co, who were supposed to be my lawyers.

I was stupid.

Afterwards, I went to discuss the BHP Billiton situation with ICAP—why had they started to do business with TMT and then stopped? I was told BHP Billiton's Australian bosses were concerned about the trades and the trader who made them was fired after internal compliance. BHP Billiton deleted all FFA transactions and cancelled all FFA trades and totally disappeared from FFA trading for three years. There will be more about this in my next book, but it was all part of the conspiracy to destabilize the commodities market and to bankrupt TMT.

It's interesting to note that, during two BHP Billiton board meetings held in Melbourne and London during October and November 2008, BHPB announced that they were quitting the pre-conditioned merger with Rio Tinto. BHPB and Rio Tinto lawyers jointly and quietly withdrew the merger application in Washington DC. So, BHP Billiton and Rio Tinto never did merge. It was all fake news—intended to do nothing more than create volatility. All evidence of the pre-conditioned merger then disappeared, to cover up the manipulation.

All the while, during these long negotiations and clogged ports and collapsing mineral and metal demands, Royal Bank of Scotland was quietly trading forward freight agreements with BHP Billiton and Rio Tinto. Fred Goodwin and his old boss Don Argus were edging their way into a shipping market that, for most people, felt too volatile to touch—and if that isn't cosy enough for you, guess who else was banking at RBS? Rio Tinto. TMT's financial department was scrutinized a few times by the RBS Asia team and reports were sent to London. These reports ended up with Fred Goodwin and Gerard Joynson, the head of futures marketing. I have access to documents from RBS to show that Today Makes Tomorrow's (my company) accounts and Rio Tinto's accounts in Singapore and Australia were opened next to each other, even though the system automatically aligns bank accounts in alphabetical order.

A note here about RBS Sempra Commodities: Sempra Commodities was a subsidiary of Sempra Energy, a US utilities holding company that was sued for market manipulation. Sempra Commodities was Sempra Energy's stake in a sudden partnership with RBS Group, formed on April 1, 2008, to "market and trade natural gas, power, petroleum, coal and base metals". The real role of this "partnership" was to create an accounting pipeline between the world's two largest banks— JPMorgan Chase in the US and Royal Bank of Scotland in the UK. Cynically, RBS was made to sell its stake in RBS Sempra Commodities by the European Commission as a condition of the UK Government's takeover of the Group in 2010. Guess who bought RBS Sempra Commodities' trading book? Why, JPMorgan Chase of course!

The bank codes of TMT, Rio Tinto, and RBS Sempra Commodities (operating commodity trading in the US) were almost touching. This meant that money could be moved quickly around the globe in a 24/7 banking system. Here's how it works—in the RBS GBM (Global Banking & Markets) computer operating systems, if you made TMT's account zero, the total money in that account would move upwards to the next account (either Rio Tinto or RBS Sempra Commodities). The money could then be withdrawn from that account and utilized for whatever purpose (to make even more money) and the original amount then replaced in TMT's account. So, basically, money can move around different accounts within the bank's internal system and the total amount on the balance sheet won't change. Manipulating a bank's computer system like this is serious fraud!

The intention was to swap cash between London (at 3:00pm) and New York (at 9:00am)—money movement that left no fingerprint. After 6:00pm in London, nobody could access bank information over the weekend—however, due to account statements being so confusing, TMT Taipei contacted Marie Chang, a lady in the FFA clearing department of RBS Singapore, who had access to a 24/7 system and this eventually led to the discovery of how RBS were manipulating TMT's account by trading with BHP Billiton. I'm still investigating this series of events and more evidence is coming to light every day. I will go into the fraud in more detail in my second book, when I have all the evidence collected.

For now, it's another piece of the jigsaw and part of the underlying theme of this book.

But let's get back to the financial crisis, in October 2008 the major banks' plan was almost complete. The VIX Index, a measure of volatility across the commodity market that's known colloquially and appropriately as the "Fear Index", spiked higher than ever before for nine consecutive days. I couldn't believe it. It seemed impossible. In August the charter rates for the largest dry bulk carriers were $200,000 a day but, by November, they were a little under $4,000 (fixed by Cargill). A crisis in the banking sector had now bled into the physical commodity market. Volatility increased the demand for liquidity which, because of credit being sucked into a black hole of bad debts and toxic assets, couldn't be met. This led to stock piling up in ports and ships floundering, half-built, in shipyards. However, because the solution was so simple and the triggers of growth still present (emerging economies and rapid globalization), the crisis was controllable—as long as there was some way of getting liquidity back into the system, so people could make good on their payments and purchase long-term orders again.

The volatility in the commodity market, the temporary closure of mines, the electronic products and tin-foil toys gathering dust in factories, suddenly moved the credit crisis from the financial sector into every sector. It forced the Federal Reserve, the US Treasury and Central Banks across the world, to forgo their trepidation about moral hazard. They quickly came to realize, if they didn't bail out the banks a myriad of industries and businesses that relied on short-term loans and easy credit, would fall too—one by one. We might be able to imagine a world without Lehman Brothers, or even without RBS or JPMorgan Chase, but could our political leaders envision a future without steel to build train stations, concrete for roads, or even cobalt for batteries? Not at all! World trade was at stake and the easiest, most immediate solution was obvious; pump cash into the banks so they could start lending again.

By November 2008, the era of Quantitative Easing (bailouts) on a mass scale was well and truly underway. The banks were scrambling to swop their toxic, previously unpurchaseable debts, assets, and obligations for sturdy, reliable, and highly liquid government bonds. They were saved. The governments assumed the burden of their losses so they'd still be financially stable enough to continue to lend money to steel manufacturers, shipping companies, and every other business that kept the market turning.

As is always the difficulty with history, it's hard to say whether or not a less volatile commodity market would have made a difference to government policy, but it's my opinion that Hank Paulson, a US Treasury Secretary whose anxieties about the dangers of moral hazard are well documented, would not have bailed out the banks to such a scale unless their failure had such far-reaching consequences.

BHP Billiton Mount Whaleback Mine

BHP Billiton CEO Marius Kloppers

THE ATM TECHNIQUE

The major financial institutions might have created enough turmoil to secure quantitative easing, but that turmoil also worsened their own positions more than they let on. It took a great deal of maneuvring to make sure they didn't collapse until the time was right. They also had to make sure the public and their elected governments never figured out exactly how bad the situation really was. To receive the cash they so desperately wanted they'd have to submit to a trial—they'd have to open their books and balance sheets to forensic accountants and financial analysts. So, the next task on the banks' to-do list was to action some "creative" accounting and "clean up" their records.

The big game changer in this was called IFRS (International Financial Reporting Standards) accounting. For over 100 years, historical accounting standards had been sufficient, then IFRS was suddenly introduced in 2005/2006 "to provide a common global language for business affairs so that company accounts are understandable and comparable across international boundaries." It was mark-to-market (M2M) accounting, or "fair value" accounting, which can lead to vastly over-valued assets, like company stocks or derivative contracts. Reason being, a company can change the value of its assets each time it issues a financial statement and record the changes as earnings.

The fact that most of the failing banks tinkered with their balance sheets to hide their debts and overemphasize their equity is well documented. RBS convinced its shareholders it was worth pouring in more money, in the form of a rights issue (when a company sells stocks to raise quick cash), less than six months before it was nationalized by the Bank of

England. It wasn't necessarily its customers' money that RBS was after, but control of their accounts, much as it was controlling TMT's account (I will provide more details of this in my next book). Even the Bank of England vastly underestimated the amount of financing the newly acquired RBS would need to get it back on its feet, because the company seemed so much healthier than it actually was. This meant that the British taxpayer was heinously overcharged for its purchase of RBS. As of 2017, almost a decade since the worst days of the financial crisis, while most banks have paid back the money they owed to governments, RBS is still in the mire. Her Majesty's government owns around 70% of RBS, which made a £7 billion loss in 2017. It hasn't quite turned out to be the investment everyone hoped for. In fact, UK banks are not expected to reach full recovery for another few years. Similarly, the European Union will take a further decade to smooth out the financial turmoil.

In the USA the banks have recovered, but financial inequality has reached a new high, with the top 1% raking in more money than ever before and the rest of the country lagging behind and struggling to pay off astronomical student debts, auto loans, and medical fees. It makes you wonder whether, if the US Treasury and the Bank of England had had the correct information about what exactly was wrong with their banks, they might have done things differently, and recovery would've happened across the board by now, not just for the jet set. But they didn't have the correct information, because RBS and JPMorgan Chase (and others like them) found a simple and effective way to cover up their many sins—me!

Or, to be more precise, my company—Today Makes Tomorrow.

I was an outsider. I was fresh—a family business and not a hedge fund nor a big corporation. I didn't have a relationship with the media. TMT was a privately owned family firm, which meant it didn't have a board of investors second-guessing its every move, and wasn't subject to the same tests and regulations as companies registered on the Stock Exchange. Like I said, I wasn't a member of the Old Boy's Club and I had, in hindsight, a naïve regard for the "honorable" traditions of the City of London. So, when Royal Bank of Scotland appeared on the scene in May 2007 and started to court me with gifts of personalized mah-jong sets and engraved stationery, I believed it to be a sign that I'd made it. I just wish I'd realized then, that their interest in having me as a client was purely Machiavellian. They weren't interested in the prosperity of TMT as a company, they were just interested in its cash.

It wasn't just RBS' global reputation of innovation and stability (laughable now) that appealed to me, but also the fact that they were so closely connected to the London Clearing House. The RBS I signed up with wasn't the same bank that any small business owner could walk into on the high street. It was a specific subsidiary of RBS Shipping, which existed under the mantle of RBS GBM (Global Banking & Markets)—an investment arm of the RBS empire. At that time RBS was the largest bank in the world and seemed to have aspirations for global dominance, displayed by its acquisition of the Dutch bank ABN AMRO in 2007, despite market warnings. It was this kind of arrogance that led, in part, to its failure.[1]

Like most client-led businesses, RBS had entire divisions whose sole purpose was to woo new account holders. These divisions were populated by some of the most charming people you would ever come across. They knew exactly how to placate your concerns, soothe your doubts, and bolster your ego, until you willingly, gratefully, signed on the dotted line. As I found to my own detriment, sometimes clients were so trusting they forgot to read the small print. That was the problem with TMT. We were, and still are, a company that does its due diligence and values attention to detail, but if someone is trying to get one over on you it's harder than

[1] RBS Shipping Centre ledger account 160101 was a house account (a bank's own personal account with another bank) with JPMorgan Chase. This will become relevant later.

you might imagine to stay vigilant, especially when they send multiple "copies" of a document to be signed, which aren't true copies at all.

It's foolishly simple, isn't it, you give someone an original contract which they examine carefully and then sign. Some time later, you send over a "copy" which you "need for your files." They're not going to read it with the same care they took with the original, are they? So, if the difference is small enough, you'll get away with it. RBS sent me many versions of documents to sign that contained discrepancies from the originals—discrepancies that even my lawyers at the time didn't notice, as they believed they were true copies. The discrepancies didn't come to light until years later, when they were pointed out by an investigative attorney. I'll never forget the moment they told me that I had, unknowingly, authorized RBS to create intermediary accounts in TMT's name—and that they had registered me as a professional investor and authorized themselves to do whatever they wanted on my behalf. The only thing that saved Today Makes Tomorrow from complete destruction was, I only signed up a subsidiary (TMT Liberia) that specifically operated tankers and managed most of the risk of trading in FFAs.

The first sum went missing only two days after I opened the account with RBS—$5 million taken out of the account without authorization and deposited into a New York account at JPMorgan Chase on July 12, 2007. To put this into historical context, less than a month later, the first victim of the financial crisis (BNP Paribas) announced that it had no more liquidity and began blocking withdrawals from certain customers. To quote Timothy Geithner from his book *Stress Test*: "Every financial crisis is a crisis of confidence. Financial systems, after all, are built on belief." Our banking system only functions if people trust the banks to look after their money and return it to them when requested. When your bank account is in credit it means you're trusting that bank with your money, which is why we call it credit—from the Latin word *credere*, which means belief.

When trust collapses, there's a run on the bank—history has shown this time and time again, most recently in England when Northern Rock asked the Bank of England for a loan on September 14, 2007. A bank can just about survive a short-term liquidity problem, but a run on the bank is far more serious because banks keep very little of their customers' money in real terms. That money is technically considered and treated as a loan to the bank. The cash a bank will dole out to, say, first-time home owners is the same cash that someone else has deposited. So, if there's a run and everyone's demanding their money immediately, the bank probably won't be able to cope. It's one of the many reasons why financial news and interviews are usually so interminably dull; the intention is not to say or do anything that might startle the markets or spook customers into a run on the banks. In some ways it's not too different from the cheery "stiff upper lip" war propaganda of Pathé News during the London Blitz—keep calm and carry on. Except, for the financial world, the Blitz never ends!

Risk never rests.

I was mistaken to place my trust in RBS. For the entire period between September 2007 and March 2008, they were stealing my money and depositing it into their house account at JPMorgan Chase. It was a TCM account, hard to notice at first because they didn't keep the money—well, not for long anyway. It was always returned quickly and, if we noticed it, which we sometimes did with the larger amounts, then they apologized and said it was an accounting error. It might surprise readers that I continued to bank with them, but remember that an institution like RBS, with headquarters in London and international renown, had my trust and, at times, my gratitude. They had access to the London Clearing House—they could further my business and consolidate my reputation in a way that the Taiwanese and Asian banks couldn't. It's hard to be taken seriously in the West if you're not part of the European or US financial elite. Having an account with RBS went some way to achieving that for TMT.

At first I believed they were simply using TMT's money to finance ABN AMRO, from October to November 2007. The purchase of ABN AMRO by RBS has gone down in financial history as one of the worst business decisions ever made, and it's a prime example of how Fred "The Shred" Goodwin, the bullish CEO of RBS, often let his ego overshadow his good sense. ABN AMRO was stuffed full of toxic assets and, given RBS' already overextended balance sheet, the combination spelled trouble. Many in the industry said the only reason why Fred Goodwin pressed ahead with the deal, even though the markets were beginning to show sure signs of an economic downturn, was because he wanted to show Barclays, who were in competition to buy ABN AMRO, that he was more powerful than them.

At the end of October 2007 TMT was given three days to pay a margin call of $103 million, or RBS threatened to provoke default on the outgoing FFA trades. A margin call of that magnitude just didn't match the market conditions at the time, which had tremendous profitable positions. It was as if they'd just plucked the figure out of the air— which was, as I later learned from my lawyers, not far from the truth. As I mentioned before, RBS simply didn't have the infrastructure in place to move swiftly in the shipping industry's derivatives market. So, when it came to margin calls, they were inputting the sums manually and often based on very little data. This gave them the excuse to blame any inconsistencies or suspicious calculations on human error. By November 2007 RBS had returned £50 million after admitting that their demands were unfounded and extortionate.

It was just the first step.

I believe now that, at the time, they were probably testing the water to see what they could get away with. It was only after they had realized how trusting and naïve we were that they ratcheted their activities up a notch and decided to use TMT's account at RBS for their next ploy.

The scam was simple, but the exploitation of international time zones was crucial to its success. TMT did business from Singapore, RBS from London and Chicago, and JPMorgan Chase from New York, which meant that, over the course of a single working day, a great deal could be achieved and huge transactions could take place without drawing too much attention.

Basically, RBS would authorize the transfer of TMT funds to their own house account at JPMorgan Chase. Since TMT was paying out of Singapore, the money arrived in London in the early morning, after which RBS moved it to JPMorgan Chase's US dollar account within RBS in New York. This account was called CHMANEK USDTCM and it was going to be an important part of the scam.

OK, this is fairly complex stuff and not too easy to understand, but I'll try to give specific details of the most outrageous examples of RBS double-dealing.

From the very beginning, with the opening signatures of Neena Birdee, we were hoodwinked into signing faked contracts that allowed RBS to handle all TMT's accounts freely and to calculate margin calls. Look at it this way, when computers communicate with each other, human beings don't need to get involved—in other words, the transactions are automatic. RBS created intermediary TMT accounts as toll gates between both sides of the swap (cash flow) they were planning. That way, they can report discrepancies as "errors" and move money around freely, so it's not going directly between the parties on either side of the swap (i.e., RBS and JPMorgan Chase). It's called "hacking" by banking insiders, because the client's money is hijacked for a short period of time and used as the bank's own money to make a profit for the bank, then the money is put back into the client's account, minus the profit.

In the case of TMT, we were needed to save the Western banking system. They needed liquidity so they could go to the central banks to print the money they needed to clean up their toxic assets. They needed the facility to swap between the hub banks in London and New York, and other banks around the world in a 24/7 banking system. TMT's intermediary accounts, set up illegally by RBS, provided that facility. TMT's money, illegally manipulated by RBS and JPMorgan chase, provided that liquidity.

In case I've already lost you, let me explain. RBS holds an account at JPMorgan, and JPMorgan holds an account at RBS. So, RBS was transferring TMT funds into their house account at JPMorgan, which was a cute idea because, to an outside eye, it looked like the money had just moved internally, but was still technically being held by RBS. They could argue that they mistakenly thought that TMT owed them service charges, or that it was a manual error, or a computer glitch. Whatever the excuse, it was easier to explain than if it had disappeared somewhere else entirely, which is exactly what happened next. RBS then moved the money from their house account at JPMorgan, to JPMorgan's US dollar account at RBS in New York. Geographically speaking, they'd moved Today Makes Tomorrow's money from Singapore to London to New York—and from TMT's account to their own.

It's a complex transaction and not easy to understand what was going on. Basically, it was an exercise in how to turn client money into the bank's own money in a criminal manipulation. However, this "ATM" couldn't work in isolation, it had to be linked to other ATMs through a unique networking system. This will be a topic in my next book.

Royal Bank of Scotland

PLAN A

Fred Goodwin (RBS CEO) bought his third phone, paid for by himself, around September 7, 2007—the same time he instructed Gerard Joynson to tell the Singapore office to send an email to TMT. Do I have any evidence that Goodwin himself gave the instruction to Gerard Joynson? Well, they both worked closely together in scamming TMT, they're both Scottish, and they look alike (as least to a Taiwanese like me they do). I was supposed to meet Joynson at RBS headquarters in May and June 2008, but I met the strange man instead, who I now believe to have been Fred Goodwin. TMT's Richard Lee arranged both meetings for me with Gerard Joynson. Joynson never showed up, yet he never contacted Richard Lee to find out what went on. Why? Because he knew. Both Joynson and Goodwin used the pseudonym Russell Goodwin and they may even be related to each other? So, no direct evidence, but I'm prepared to stick my neck out and say 'yes, he did.'

Anyway, the email read "Please remit the money to RBOSGB2RTCM," in BOLD letters, copied to RBS Singapore group mail. However, the initial agreement TMT entered into with RBS gave the Swift Code as RBOSGB2L— normally, clients use 2L (it's the same with Barclays, HBOS, Lloyds, etc.), it's rare for clients to send money to a TCM account—but this was Royal Bank of Scotland, the largest bank in the world for God's sake. What could be wrong with it? After that TMT remitted all funds to RBOSGB2RTCM, which was RBS' own house account. I wonder who included in the Singapore group mail? A good guess would be James Travis and Neena Birdee—RBS' very own 007 and Bond girl, sent from London to spy and then called back to London to report their findings.

RBS applied for emergency cash via JPMorgan Chase on the same time horizon (March 13, 2008) that the New York Federal Reserve first approved Section 13(3) of the Federal Reserve Act to lend to "any individual, partnership or corporation in unusual and exigent circumstances"—in other words, to organizations outside the usual remit of Fed lending. However, to receive those funds they needed $484 million of their own money as equity. They didn't have it. To make matters worse, the second financial quarter of 2008 was coming up fast and they'd have to open their books again. On March 20, 2008, I attempted to withdraw $10 million to send to two separate accounts at different banks, which should have been available immediately. Strangely, only half that money turned up and the other $5 million didn't appear until April 2. RBS said they sent me a receipt of payment (confirming that the payment was made) via JPMorgan, but it never arrived. Some people at TMT suspected that JPMorgan might have faked the Swift payment confirmation (which is the most recognized means of tracking international payments, almost identical to an IBAN code). But why? $5 million isn't a vast amount of money for a global bank. Why couldn't they pay it? Why did they have to resort to faking the payment confirmation?

Because RBS had no liquidity at all!

It's like this; the banks could make totally ridiculous margin calls and the client would have to pay, otherwise it was sudden death. Over six months TMT had remitted a total of $484 million to the RBS designated account RBOSGB2RTCM—the missing $5 million was used by RBS to open the account with JPMorgan Chase's equity division in New York (I'm convinced this is connected to the Fairfield Sentry Fund, as Bernie Madoff confirmed that $5 million was the minimum amount needed to open an account). So, when the money was paid into RBOSGB2RTCM, it looked like RBS' own money to the outsider—this was fraud!

The RBS house account switched the cash to JPMorgan Chase account CHMANEK USDTCM, which transferred the money to the RBS Shipping Centre in New York, so the Fed thought it was JPMorgan Chase's own money and it was used to buy securities that were eligible to receive PDCF funding from the Federal Reserve. It was still morning in New York when all this happened and RBS now had money to spend on financial products or securities that would be worth 25 times what they paid for them by the afternoon—as long as they could palm them off on the Fed. After they'd not only made back the money they had stolen, but had also multiplied it by 25, RBS returned it to TMT in Singapore and told the accountants who noticed the missing funds that it was an internal error. In a nutshell, it was a swap agreement that left no footprint, unlike the more commonly used Swift money transactions (all client money must be transferred via Swift, so there's a record of it). Consequently, what RBS did was illegal, as the money they were transferring was client money and not the bank's own funds.

Let me reiterate what I said in the previous chapter. Computers and their automatic transactions are the key. RBS illegally "borrowed" TMT's money and used intermediary accounts to "loan" that money to JPMorgan Chase. JPMorgan Chase then bought toxic financial products with TMT's money and took those toxic products to the New York Federal Reserve, who bought them from JPMorgan Chase for 25 times what JPMC paid for them. Once the "borrowed" funds came back to RBS, they put the money back into TMT's account. The keys to this scam are the intermediary accounts, so the money manipulation can't be traced directly to the banks on either side of the swap—or, if it is, it can be put down to "human error." But the banks' computer systems ensure the transactions can be done quickly, utilizing the 24/7 international banking timetable so that, hopefully, they won't be noticed.

It's quite simple really, when you think about it.

The $11.1 billion RBS eventually received from the PDCF, via JPMorgan Chase, was most of the $12.1 billion bailout from the Federal Reserve and, without it, it's unlikely that RBS would've survived between March and June 2008. But it wasn't a gift, it was a loan that had to be repaid; so Fred "The Shred" Goodwin decided to raise a rights issue— that traditional way for a troubled company to raise cash from its investors. The basic principle is, they offer their investors the opportunity to buy more shares at a special discount for a limited period. The number of shares available aren't unlimited, but specific to each investor in proportion to how many they already own. This is so the value of the stock isn't diluted. RBS successfully raised the money on June 6, which, I believe, they used to pay back the loan to JPMorgan Chase.

What happened to the spare $1 billion of Fed money?

On March 14 Jamie Dimon, the CEO of JPMorgan Chase, called an ex-colleague at Bear Stearns and discovered they were in serious trouble. Bear Stearns, one of the stalwarts of Wall Street and an investment bank that, like many others, might have looked more like a casino to the outside eye, was about to declare bankruptcy. It had dived straight into the mortgage-backed securities craze and, by late 2007, had begun to reap the consequences and didn't have enough equity to outweigh its risks. It had a strong reputation, mostly because it survived the Great Depression without firing a single employee. It might have been the smallest of Wall Street's infamous five investment banks, but its imminent collapse was taken very seriously.

Interesting to note that the JPMorgan Chase building and the Bear Stearns building were next to each other on Park Avenue.

Jamie Dimon was in a better place than most to help because, unlike other gung-ho CEOs, he'd been preparing for a financial recession for some time. He was one of the powerful few who saw the storm coming. So, he arranged to buy Bear Stearns. It's fairly logical to conclude that JPMorgan

Chase might have used that $1 billion to secure a $30 billion loan from the NY Federal Reserve, which would serve to underwrite Bear Stearns' more dangerous assets (those pesky CDOs again) and seal a deal to purchase Bear Stearns for only $2 a share, don't you think? Anyway, the price was a shocking one-tenth of its market price only two days prior. JPMorgan Chase bought Bear Stearns for the bargain sum of $1.2 billion which, according to the *New York Times*, was a third of the price at which Bear Stearns went public in 1985, and that's not even considering inflation—along with, of course, the $30 billion the Fed agreed to pay to cover the toxic assets. It was cut-throat deals like this, and desperate decisions made over long weekends to try to prevent panic when the markets opened on Monday, that made JPMorgan Chase a beneficiary of the financial crisis. For a few years they were one of the few lifeboats available. The problem was, as we'll see, when they didn't extend the hand of help, all hell broke loose.

Back to Royal Bank of Scotland. Over ten months, between 2007 and 2008, RBS managed to write off $900 billion in assets from their audited balance sheet, using this scam. It's there, plain as day. If you look at their financial statement from 2007 going into 2008, it shrinks from $4 trillion to $3.1 trillion. In case there's any confusion, a balance sheet doesn't just count a company's assets, but also its debts, and having a very large balance sheet is usually a sign of trouble. It was a huge amount of toxic assets and debt to disappear in just ten months, given that it was a time when nobody was really making any money, especially not RBS. It was 20% of their assets and liabilities. I find it surprising that such an obvious sign of fraud has yet to be investigated by the regulators, or picked up by economists or investigative journalists.

So, that's why RBS needed to hijack TMT's account. They had no liquidity and had to use someone else's money to fund their fraud.

The Primary Dealer Credit Facility mechanism so blatantly exploited by RBS, was initiated in March 2008 after the collapse of Bear Stearns alerted the US government to the severity of the financial crisis. Simply put, the PDCF was a way of loaning to the banks. It allowed them to register as primary dealers and sell their toxic assets (known in this context as securities) to the Federal Reserve in exchange for funds. In financial-speak, we say they sold those securities through the "Fed's discount window," which just means they got a way better price from the Federal Reserve than they would on the market. The PDCF was a loan because the banks promised to buy back the securities at a later specified date for the same price at which they had sold them, not at market value. It was a way for banks to get good, cheap liquidity while the Fed had some collateral, even if it wasn't worth much.

Royal Bank of Scotland and JPMorgan Chase co-ordinated their efforts to test the system. The big banks had already created volatility on the commodities market; sub-prime mortgages were coming to the end of their teaser rates; defaults were gathering momentum; a crash was coming; the banks knew this because they'd engineered it. They were hoping the PDCF was just the forerunner of TARP and the era of quantitative easing around the world—the fruition of their Plan A. But they had to be sure—what if it didn't work? They needed a Plan B.

That was me!

I'm not doubting the efficacy of the Federal Reserve's policies—it made sense and it worked. But, by purchasing those securities for more than their market value, they undoubtedly created an opportunity for unscrupulous bankers to make a profit on the basic principle of buying low and selling high. Through the PDCF the Federal Reserve of New York loaned tens of billions of dollars a day during the crisis.

Meanwhile, at Today Makes Tomorrow it was business as usual—or as usual as it could be during the greatest financial upheaval since the Great Depression. We had no idea that TMT's account had been used to raise funds through the Primary Dealer Credit Facility, fund the liquidity of ABN

AMRO, or that we were even remotely connected to the last-minute purchase of Bear Stearns.

On June 2, 2008, four days after my mysterious meetings with the strange man in the deserted offices in Bishopsgate, RBS was set to receive a £12 billion injection from its successfully raised rights issue. An injection of cash that, if you remember, they desperately needed to pay off the $11.1 billion loan from JPMorgan Chase via the Federal Reserve. I now believe that those two meetings in the deserted offices of RBS were, in fact, set up by Fred Goodwin to discover how much more they could get away with. They wanted to find out how much I'd noticed. They wanted to know whether or not I was suspicious about the money disappearing and reappearing in my account, or whether I'd started to ask questions about how exactly the crippling margin calls that TMT was being subjected to were being calculated.

I now suspect, having seen his face emblazoned across the front page of the *Financial Times*, that the man in the blue suit was Fred Goodwin himself. I believe the infamous control-freak wanted to see how his plan was working out at ground level. RBS had already sent teams to inspect my offices and computer systems and discover how TMT ran its bookkeeping and its operations in Taiwan and Asia. They knew which floors did what in the TMT building and they sent a faked contract, created in New York, to the second floor, knowing there was nothing there but a library and that all mail should go to the eighth floor. So they'd have known pretty much all there was to know by early 2008. Maybe Fred Goodwin needed to confirm that I really was as naïve as people said, before he felt comfortable executing the next part of the plan. I'm sure the RBS people who came to the TMT offices took a lot of information away without being authorized to do so, and they may very well have hacked TMT's computers as well—all to allow Fred Goodwin to:

a) Instruct my law firm, Ince & Co, to switch my lawyer to cover up evidence

b) Instruct shipping to file a Rule B attachment through Petros Pappas

c) Instruct the manipulation of Vantage shares

d) Instruct the opening of a JPMorgan Chase account for Vantage shares.

This book will show how it all came together.

The next part of the plan was twofold. The grand scheme was to make money from AIG's imminent failure, which would eventually happen on September 16, 2008, but which, no doubt, the data-crunching inmates of the financial markets saw coming by that summer. However, to achieve their goal, RBS was going to need TMT's accounts once again and then, after the plan had been seen through to its natural conclusion, they were going to need TMT to default and disappear.

Taking the evidence of the scam with it.

JPMorgan Chase

LEHMAN BROTHERS

A few years ago I met Dick Fuld. People remember him as the "Gorilla" CEO of Lehman Brothers at the time of the financial crash. He was everything that was wrong with the banking system in those early years following the millennium; a testosterone-driven gambler, infamous for his anger issues and terrified workforce. That's where he got the nickname "Gorilla" and he was so proud of it he installed a real, stuffed gorilla in his office. He came to represent the worst excesses and moral failings of Wall Street. Google him and you'll see a series of photographs in which he stares, belligerently, into the camera lens like he's looking for a fight. He probably is! That's the kind of man Dick Fuld was in his heyday.

Not that he's mellowed at all since his fall from grace. The media most often describe him as "unapologetic" in the many articles that have been written since the crash, labeling him as one of the top five, top ten, top 20 people to blame for it. You can watch clips of his Congressional hearings online, and I recommend it, not only for some pretty spectacular throwdowns, but also to get an idea of what a formidable character Fuld is. My personal favorite is his encounter with John Mica, the Republican Representative for Florida.

Mica says to Fuld, 'If you haven't discovered your role, you're the villain.'

Fuld replies with a sneer, 'That's a matter for your committee.'

When I watched him during the hearing, and later when I met him in person, I felt uncannily aware that, underneath a mask of impassivity, there burned a fire of cold rage, which I hoped wouldn't emerge for me to experience at firsthand. He spoke slowly, carefully, with the patronizing timbre of a teacher reprimanding a slightly dim schoolboy. If anyone dared to disagree with him in his Lehman days, then this chastising tone would deepen and slow until, as the saying goes, you became aware that you were in the eye of the storm and that soon all hell was going to break loose.

At Lehman Brothers he was respected and feared. After all, by the time of the crash, he'd been working there for 40 years. He started in the late sixties, which is more than a decade before the Big Bang. In the financial world the Big Bang doesn't refer to the explosive singularity that marked the birth of our known universe and everything in it—no, as I said in Chapter 2, it refers to the deregulation of the City of London during the 1980s. Back then, before the Big Bang, a financial crash like the one in 2008 could never have happened, because rating agencies like Standard & Poor, Moody's, and Fitch Ratings were paid for by the buyer, not the issuer. A rating agency is the body that decides what "tranche" the debt belongs in, in other words, how risky it is. If the owners of the debt are timely and regular with their repayments, then the debt is AAA but, if they sometimes struggle to make it, then that's B grade or, as bankers affectionately call it, "junk."

In the various accounts written about the whys and hows of the financial crash in succeeding years, the large rating agencies are always selected as one of the prime causes of the sub-prime mortgage bubble. CDOs—the craze for buying up bags of civilian debt and receiving their repayments, in return for promising the mortgage broker that you'll pay out if they default—rely heavily on rating agencies. If these rating agencies work for the potential buyer of the CDO then, of course, they're going to want to be as accurate and discriminating as possible regarding the quality of the debt. If they told a buyer that a B grade was actually AAA, then they'd be sued and lose a large chunk, if not all, of their clientele. However, when they were being paid by the issuer, it got to be a whole new story. The issuer is the company that provides the debt to be turned into a CDO. So, in order to get as much revenue as possible,

they're going to want their debt to be graded as quality, even if
it isn't. If a rating agency is too harsh, or maybe too accurate
with its grading system, then it's likely the issuer will move
to a different, laxer firm. Immediately, the incentive changes.
Rating agencies that were rewarded for accuracy were now
rewarded for giving over-generous estimations.

As you can imagine, this eventually led to the AAA grade
CDOs traded in 2007 being full of B grade junk. The buyers
had no idea what they were buying and the issuers didn't care.
The issuers were, of course, investment banks like Dick Fuld's
Lehman Brothers.

This wasn't the only change Dick Fuld saw. Huge bonuses,
the rise of corporate "entertainment"—in which strippers
and recreational drug use became part and parcel of wooing
clients—and mathematical geniuses creating complicated
financial products that nobody else properly understood,
all led to investment banking losing its staid reputation and
becoming a breeding ground for profligate greed.

One of the most infuriating aspects of Dick Fuld's post-
Lehman career isn't the fact that he escaped with almost half
a billion dollars and no criminal record, but that, in speeches
since the crash, he's categorically refused to accept his share
of blame and, instead, criticizes the US government's policy
of encouraging home ownership. However, despite Dick
Fuld's personal failings and unlikable character, I can't help
but think that, when it came to how the crisis played out, he
was the fall guy.

Hank Paulson, the US Treasury Secretary, was known
to dislike Fuld. In the small, homogenous world of high
finance, you probably couldn't find two more different
characters. Hank Paulson is a Christian Scientist and ex
Boy Scout, who genuinely believed that the free market,
when properly functioning, attained some level of
moral beauty—a system which allowed the talented and
ambitious to succeed and trickle the wealth down to those
less fortunate. Dick Fuld represented exactly the kind

of irresponsible behavior that Hank Paulson was afraid the bailouts would encourage. Added to that, Dick Fuld and Hank Paulson were old rivals in business, from when Paulson was CEO of Goldman Sachs.

At the time of Lehman's failure the US Treasury, as represented by Hank Paulson, and the New York Federal Reserve, under Timothy Geithner and his chairman Ben Bernanke, had already provided funds to facilitate JPMorgan Chase's acquisition of Bear Stearns and the bailing out of the government sponsored enterprises Fannie Mae and Freddie Mac. While these moves were heavily criticized by the public, it set a precedent that led Dick Fuld to assume he could rely on the government for help. This led him to reject the Korea Development Bank's offer of $23 a share for his company. In fact, some say he didn't start working on finding a buyer for Lehman Brothers until far too late in the game, because he was sure the government would lend a helping hand. Two days before Lehman filed for bankruptcy, he called Hank Paulson and begged for help.

'If you would give us a bridge, we can wind down these positions and make a lot of this ugliness go away.'

Paulson abruptly told him the help he'd expected wasn't going to come.

The weekend before Lehman declared bankruptcy (September 12–15), the Federal Reserve expanded the PDCF, allowing banks to pledge new types of collateral in return for overnight capital. Short-term loans were how Lehman Brothers had been funding themselves for a while and Dick Fuld knew this extension of the PDCF could solve all his problems and move Lehman's condition from critical to stable. Infuriatingly, this extension was offered to many banks and institutions, but not to Lehman Brothers. When Fuld tried to get in touch with Timothy Geithner, chairman of the NY Fed at the time (and, after Barak Obama's inauguration, to replace Hank Paulson as Treasury Secretary) he found himself being blackballed.

Dick Fuld now had two days to turn the recently floated proposal of a Barclays acquisition into a reality. Bob Diamond, the CEO of Barclays and an American himself who was keen to prove that his bank was equal to the bull-market reputation of Wall Street, was very interested. Or he seemed to be. That deal fell through at the eleventh hour after the British government and their financial regulatory advisory body at the time (FSA) refused to back it, or to provide any funds towards it. Bob Diamond was hoping he could rely on their help to offset some of Lehman's more toxic assets, much as the Fed did for JPMorgan Chase's acquisition of Bear Stearns. But the British were too busy putting out their own financial fires to consider, even for a second, taking on one of America's most notorious investment banks.

I find it strange that the British government's disapproval only came to light on Lehman's last Sunday in business. It's stranger still that Bob Diamond was so optimistic about the deal, without having secured their approval first. The Financial Crisis Inquiry Commission pressed an executive at Lehman Brothers on precisely that question—how was it that no one had asked the FSA (the biggest financial regulator in the UK until 2013) for approval, given that their cooperation was essential to the deal? His only response was that he "agreed."

It was, to quote the examination, "nuts."

The next day (Monday, September 15) Lehman Brothers filed for bankruptcy and the world was shocked by images and newsreels of bankers pouring out onto the streets of Manhattan, clutching cardboard boxes full of framed photographs, potted plants, and personal effects. Looking back at those iconic pictures now, what's most striking is the look of profound shock and confusion in their eyes as they suddenly found themselves plunged into a world where an institution like Lehman could fail. It was shock and confusion that rippled round the world. Headlines spelled it out:

"LEHMAN CRASH SENDS SHOCKWAVES ROUND WORLD"

"MELTDOWN MONDAY"

"BANKING QUAKE"

"CITY BRACED FOR JOBS BLOODBATH"

And, perhaps the most prosaic:

"THE BROTHERS GRIMM"

It was, after all, the first real casualty of the financial crisis. The others, from Northern Rock to Bear Stearns, had all been bailed out or guided into mutually beneficial mergers. As *The Guardian* reported a year later "Lehman was the biggest bankruptcy in US history." Pundits all over the world turned their gaze towards the West and began to wonder whether they were seeing the end of the global financial system as they knew it. Russia shut down its stock exchange; the British bank HBOS had its value halved within an hour; AIG began to teeter on the brink; Goldman Sachs suffered a 14% drop in its stock; Morgan Stanley lost a quarter of its value. People began to realize that perhaps you couldn't just allow the banks to fail in the belief that the market would right itself without too much detrimental effect on the economy. They began to see how incestuously entangled financial institutions had become, so that when one failed, everyone got hurt.

That week, public opinion shifted dramatically. They'd seen what could happen if even the smallest investment bank on Wall Street failed—imagine what the effect on the global economy would be if AIG, or Goldman Sachs, or JPMorgan Chase also failed! Moral hazard was on the way out. The death of Lehman Brothers proved to the world that quantitative easing (bailouts) was the only viable solution. The Federal Reserve, the US Treasury, the Bank of England, the European Central Bank, all changed tack that week. They stopped poking their heads into the sand and scrambled for ways to pump liquidity into the system, with the urgency of paramedics in a traffic jam. To this day people are more likely to ask why Lehman Brothers wasn't bailed out, rather than ask why the others were.

It was the collapse of Lehman that precipitated the reign of quantitative easing and proved once and for all that the major financial institutions were, indeed "too big to fail." It was also responsible for getting the CEOs of the surviving banks exactly what they wanted—a relatively consequence-free injection of cash right when they needed it. Dick Fuld's fall led to their continuing rise. If Lehman Brothers hadn't collapsed, if the deal with Barclays had gone through, or even if they hadn't tumbled from grace quite so rapidly and had time to streamline their books, then would the US, UK, and EU Central Banks have been so quick to provide unlimited liquidity to its competitors and cohorts? My guess is, probably not! It took an example like Lehman to show how close the financial system was to a long-term and painful depression.

How convenient!

This is what we know: Dick Fuld was, even for a Wall Street banker, disliked; that certain people believed Hank Paulson needed to be shocked out of his adherence to the principle of moral hazard; that insiders saw the failure of Lehman coming for a while.

We have Larry McDonald (a Lehman vice-president) on record saying, 'They put Lehman Brothers to sleep. They executed her. They put a pillow over her face.'

Put all that together and you have the makings of a convincing argument that the failure of Lehman wasn't only foreseen, but was also encouraged.

In the bankruptcy filing, Lehman's lawyer Harvey Miller said, 'The real tragedy is, we missed TARP by a week.'

I'd argue that TARP, the government's Troubled Asset Relief Program he was referring to, would never have happened if it wasn't for Lehman's failure.

On September 10 Jamie Dimon at JPMorgan Chase had issued a $7.5 billion margin call to Lehman, which completely exhausted their cash reserve and pushed them over the brink. If the stability of the markets was JPMorgan Chase's primary concern, why would they take such an extreme action? I believe they wanted Lehman Brothers to fail, and fail rapidly.

After Lehman declared bankruptcy it was broken up and sold off to Barclays and the Japanese holding company Nomura—that's the same Barclays that somehow forgot to check if the FSA would approve their purchase, and whose last-minute back-out of the merger left Lehman floundering with no choice but to file for Chapter 11 bankruptcy. They ended up with exactly what they wanted, but at a hefty discount. They purchased Lehman's North America operations for $1.75 billion, including its Manhattan office and 9,000 employees. The Manhattan office alone was valued at $1 billion (Dick Fuld said $1.5 billion). At the time, many complained that the sale was being rushed through so fast they had no way to determine whether or not Barclays was paying a fair price. At the bankruptcy court Lehman declared $639 billion in assets—so why were they bankrupted? Obviously because a scapegoat was needed to camouflage the "rescue" of AIG and start the game of musical "save the banks" chairs for the Western financial establishment.

Nomura purchased Lehman's Asian division and parts of the European division for $225 million—the price was so low because it acquired employees, not assets. Nomura hardly features at all in popular accounts of the financial crisis because they're seen as nothing more than a small foreign bank who happened to pick up a slice of Lehman during the fire sale. I disagree. I think their purchase plays a central role in uncovering the true events. If Barclays had been allowed to buy Lehman Brothers that weekend, then Nomura would, obviously, not have had a look in. The division Nomura was interested in would have gone to Barclays. Given that, you'd say Nomura couldn't have known the Barclays deal was going to fall through, wouldn't you? So, how were they so ready to buy up the Asian division? I've lived in Tokyo for most of my life and I understand the culture and practices of the Japanese far better than the vast majority of Western financial journalists—there's no way Nomura would make such a large acquisition in such a short space of time. They would've done their due diligence; they would've costed it carefully and jumped through all the hoops—and been fully aware of what they were taking on. That's how Nomura works. For this reason I think that Nomura, and therefore Barclays, knew well in advance that the deal was going to fall through and that Lehman would file for bankruptcy.

The demise of Lehman Brothers

Dick Fuld on Twitter?

AIG

The American International Group (AIG) was the fifth institution to be bailed out during the financial crisis. In fact, AIG had to be bailed out multiple times, to the eventual tune of $182 billion, making it the biggest bailout in history. To make matters even worse, AIG isn't even a bank—it shouldn't, technically speaking, have qualified for government aid from the Federal Reserve at all. In order to save AIG the Fed had to use an old clause of their Powers Act known as Section 13(3), which was last used to give US airlines emergency funding in the wake of 9/11, so they could weather market reaction to the terror attack. AIG is considered by many experts as the first solid proof that, during the financial crisis, some institutions were, indeed "too big to fail."

It was a company riddled with bad decisions, an overblown risk-taking culture, sloppy accounting, and dangerously low levels of equity. However, the Federal Reserve was not really responsible for regulating AIG since it wasn't a bank, and not responsible for resolving its bankruptcy. At least, that's how it should have been. But AIG's various misguided investments in sub-prime mortgage securities bound it inexorably to the big banks. The Federal Reserve feared that the failure of AIG could provoke a chain reaction across Wall Street that would have the potential to cripple the US economy. It seems that others had also recognized this privileged position of AIG because, in the days leading up to its failure, two things were happening—the first, and perhaps the most important, was Goldman Sachs shorting (speculative selling of securities) the market.

In his book *Inside Job* Charles Ferguson states:

> *They had played AIG for such a massive sucker while shorting the mortgage market that by 2008 they knew that their shorts alone could precipitate AIG's collapse. And what did Goldman do about that? Push ever harder, while shorting AIG, of course.*

Goldman Sachs used its influence to call in debts they knew AIG couldn't pay and, therefore, provoked its untimely default while, at the same time, shorting them and making a profit from that default. Goldman weren't the only ones who spotted the rats fleeing the ship and who saw they could make a profit from the destruction of an American insurance giant. Many other large US banks, and European banks too, were marking down AIG's derivatives so aggressively that they were unable to sell any of their assets. No one was touching anything AIG had to offer. The market turned against it. Rumors spread like wildfire across the global marketplace and AIG stock plummeted.

It was clear they'd been writing CDSs left, right, and center for over 25 massive financial institutions throughout the world. AIG took on the risk for the interest. They didn't expect the irresponsibly rated AAA super-senior tranches of CDOs to default, so they racked up $80 billion worth of CDSs. But the mortgage bond market was fraudulent—the banks were preying on the American people and their dreams of owning a home. When the sub-prime mortgage bubble burst the CDOs did default and, when they did, AIG's rating was downgraded. When that happened, people started to call in their CDSs, no longer trusting AIG to insure their risk after all.

AIG suddenly found itself being asked to pay out large sums that it simply didn't have and was forced, in mid-September—less than a week after Lehman Brothers' historic collapse—to start bankruptcy proceedings. Luckily, or unluckily as some AIG shareholders have argued, they never had to actually declare bankruptcy, as the Federal Reserve bailed them out to the tune of $85 billion, in return for 80% of their equity. AIG was saved! However, a great deal of the

US government's money quickly by-passed AIG and went straight to counterparties based in foreign countries, making the benefit to the US economy questionable.

Christopher Dodd, chairman for the Senate Banking Committee, commented, 'It is not clear who we are rescuing.'

Those counterparties included the French bank Société Générale, the German Deutsche Bank, the Swiss UBS, Barclays in England, the Bank of Montreal in Canada, the Dutch Rabobank, and many others.

You're probably saying this is just one more example of taxpayers' money bailing out a financial institution, only to see their hard-earned cash going to the big banks and into the pockets of the same people who caused the mess in the first place. You could say it's just another case of the 1% benefitting from their close ties to the political elite, instead of that 99% who had actually paid benefitting in the form of small business loans, mortgages, and a working economy. And you'd be right! But, during my years of research, I began to piece together a suspicion that there was a lot more going on.

My theory regarding the AIG bailout and the role played by some of out best-known institutions is, at this point, unproven and nothing more than an informed hunch. However, with that disclaimer out of the way, let me paint you a picture of just what might have happened.

Essentially, at the heart of my theory lies that old devil, the credit default swap (CDS). I haven't fully explored or explained this financial device yet, so allow me to do so now. The CDS had only been around for a very short time (invented by Blythe Masters from JPMorgan in 1994) when, in 2008, it exacerbated the collapse of the sub-prime mortgage bubble. The very nature of the CDS meant that, not only were the losses worsened when a CDO defaulted (when the various debtors the CDO consisted of were no longer able to pay), but they were also spread out, affecting more people and businesses than the original deal warranted (either the original mortgage or the big CDO package). In 2004 the value of the

CDS market was about $6 trillion, by the end of 2007 it had boomed to over $60 trillion That's because it was seen to be a fairly safe way for an investor to protect against default.

The seller of a CDS takes on the credit risk of the CDS buyer, who owns some underlying debt, like mortgage-backed securities. It's similar to insurance because it provides the buyer with protection against default. The seller will get a periodic protection fee (spread), similar to an insurance premium, and they're only obliged to pay out if there's a default, which is a simplistic way of putting it. In actual fact, CDSs are the most widely used credit derivative and can be used to transfer the credit risk of bonds, securities, or corporate debt, to protect against defaults, downgrades, or any other negative credit event. If the value of the principal investment falls, then the seller must pay the buyer, whatever that investment was expected to realize. So, you can see why they're useful in a situation where an investment is risky but the original investor doesn't want to sell it outright.

CDSs are also used by speculators to bet on how a CDO or, in the case of AIG, an institution, will fare for a specified period. If you think a company will survive, then you sell the CDS; if you think it's going to fail, then you buy it. To make matters more complicated, you can even buy securities that you know will fail, get a CDS with it and, that way, you'll get the interest, even if the security defaults. Speculation has grown to be the most common function for CDSs. The market for CDSs is over-the-counter and unregulated and they often get traded so much that it's hard to know who stands at each end of the transaction. Downturns in the market can cause massive defaults and risk buyers not being able to meet their obligations. Tricky isn't it?

It's a bit of a wonder to financial journalists and media groups as to how Goldman Sachs managed to emerge from AIG's astronomic failure without a scratch. By all rights, when AIG fell, Goldman Sachs should at least have wobbled. You may think the fact they didn't is a good thing and something to be celebrated. And you'd be right, if it wasn't for the story Goldman Sachs have been telling. Since the crash they've reiterated, again and again, that, unlike their competitors, they made the right and sensible decision and hadn't embroiled themselves in AIG's risky CDOs. This is, of course, a lie— if other institutions were making money on those CDOs, is it really believable to think that Goldman Sachs was just going to sit back at a safe distance? No, the truth is, up until 2007 Goldman Sachs and AIG had had a "long and fruitful relationship." AIG insured the mortgage securities that Goldman Sachs needed and it was only when the first major signs of a financial crash trickled through that Goldman Sachs started pulling away.

In fact, Goldman Sachs pulled out of its mutually beneficial relationship with AIG so fast and so openly (the short-selling referred to earlier) that many top investors and employees at AIG blame Goldman for its failure. As I've said before, the market is a delicate instrument and one nasty rumor, if spread far enough, can destroy a company. Think of it like a run on a bank, but with stocks instead of cash. Not only that, but Goldman Sachs began demanding more and more money to cover the tumbling value of the securities it had underwritten from AIG. So, AIG had even less liquidity during a credit crunch than it might have reasonably expected. In this instance, I actually believe Goldman Sachs did behave sensibly and responsibly—they had their own investors and clients to take care of. The only part that doesn't sit well with me is the question of where they purchased their various CDSs and insurances against AIG.

In 2007 Goldman Sachs began buying credit insurance (of which a CDS is a form because, remember, you're insuring against a securities failure) against AIG from many large banks, one of which was JPMorgan Chase. You might wonder why anyone would be willing to sell a CDS on AIG at that time, since selling a CDS amounts to agreeing to pay out in the event of a default—and it wasn't a secret that AIG was on the brink of a big ratings downgrade. The truth is, most banks were on both sides of the deal. They simultaneously bought and sold CDSs, thus hedging their bets so, no matter what happened, they were never completely out of pocket. Selling CDSs on AIG to Goldman Sachs was probably just a normal part of being on both sides of the deal. But Goldman Sachs was no longer on both sides of the deal, they were betting a lot that AIG would default.

They weren't wrong!

AIG, unlike everyone else, wasn't hedging anything. They were selling insurance, but never bought any so, when bonds started defaulting, they suddenly had to pay out without anyone paying in. Then people began to worry that maybe AIG wouldn't be able to afford to pay out. Moody's, a credit-rating agency, downgraded AIG's rating after they realized this and that, in turn, meant that AIG had to put up more collateral, so had less liquidity to pay out with. It's been ten years since the financial crash and the shift in our perceptions that it entailed, but we can't forget that, up until 2007–2008, AIG was solid. It was more than solid. If you wanted the safest insurance in the world, you got it from AIG. This is part of the reason why so many banks were willing to sell CDSs on AIG, because they probably couldn't quite believe that a solid-as-a-rock institution like that could ever default.

Towards the end of August RBS sold a CDS on a large portfolio of CDOs, worth $85 billion, held by AIG, to Barclays, who then resold it to JPMorgan Chase and Goldman Sachs. This CDS was issued for five years and it insured the owners (eventually Goldman Sachs) against AIG's bankruptcy. If AIG went bust Goldman received $85 billion from the British banks. At the time, this seemed like a good deal to the US banks because they were working under the assumption that the UK economy was more stable and less exposed than the US economy. I believe this CDS was part of a back-up plan, in case their attempts to prove themselves "too big to fail" didn't pull through.

I'll explain more about this and the central role played by Lehman Brothers in a later chapter. But right now I'm talking about Plan B—this credit default swap of epic proportions. The trouble with hindsight is, we now see the bailout of AIG as inevitable when, in fact, it went against historic tradition. AIG isn't a bank, not even in the way Morgan Stanley and Goldman Sachs aren't technically banks, regulated by the Federal Reserve. It's an insurance company and, yes, while its failure would have cost the financial system countless billions, and possibly more banks would have failed, public opinion was largely against the bailout. People realized it was a "back-door" deal. By the time of its failure AIG owed billions to banks, large corporations, and even states (over $12 billion of the Fed's funds went to 20 separate states in the USA). If AIG was allowed to go under, then all those people would be out of pocket. If the banks and corporations didn't get the money AIG owed them, they might fail too, and if they failed then banks and corporations they owed money to could fail as well.

Domino effect!

So, the US Treasury took one look at AIG and realized they could be watching the very first in a series of financial explosions. They figured it would be cheaper and more politically astute to save the first domino, rather than allow the whole sequence to come tumbling down. It's hard to argue with that, but it means the AIG bailout had less to do with AIG and more to do, as always, with saving the big banks.

Given that the US Treasury had, the same week AIG needed funds, let Lehman Brothers fail after a merger with Barclays fell through, why would anyone bet their life that AIG would be helped where a large investment bank, with arguably more right to be saved than an insurance company, hadn't? What's more, the possibility of Lehman's failure had been discussed by the Fed and top CEOs for weeks so, while AIGs problems arose suddenly by comparison, the mood was still dictated by Hank Paulson's well-documented philosophy of moral hazard. There was a chance that the failure of

Lehman would dispel the myth that some institutions were "too big to fail." Banking on AIG's bailout was, consequently, a risk. In the financial world, where there's a risk, there has to be insurance against it.

Plan B!

AIG logo

Hank Greenberg—CEO of AIG

PLAN B

So, now we know why Barclays, and later JPMorgan Chase and Goldman Sachs, wanted to purchase a CDS on a big portfolio of AIG's CDOs. They knew they'd benefit and receive funds if AIG was bailed out, but they wanted to protect themselves in case it wasn't. The question is, where did this CDS, originally sold to Barclays by RBS, come from?

Here's where we return to my company, Today Makes Tomorrow, and the role I unwittingly played in Plan B. The CDS issued by RBS was, believe it or not, backed by assets owned by TMT.

As I've already mentioned, the reason a UK bank issued the CDS was because the buyers assumed that, should AIG fail, US banks would be so badly affected they wouldn't be able to make good on the contract, making it worthless and destroying the issuing company. They believed UK banks would stay strong and, even if they didn't, the Bank of England had shown swift and generous action in bailing out Northern Rock in September 2007, setting a trustworthy precedent for the solidity of the British banking system.

RBS probably realized the nature of the strong market for a CDS on AIG and, most likely, thought that since AIG would be bailed out by the Federal Reserve it was a good way to make some money. If AIG was bailed out and saved they wouldn't have to pay out and would still receive the commission and profits on the CDOs. Of course, if AIG wasn't bailed out they'd owe the buyers of the CDS $85 billion (luckily for them, that didn't happen).

There was one slight problem, RBS didn't have the equity to create a CDS of that size. In order to make the grand promise that it could insure such a large portfolio of CDOs against default, it would need a huge lump sum of collateral—way more than it had to spare. RBS wanted to take this gamble because, at the time, it was sinking fast. In fact, it'd only be a month after AIG's bailout that RBS would be nationalized by the Bank of England. They were desperate. They were willing to take one last big gamble but, like every addict at the end of their game, they needed to scrounge together a stake first.

OK, time to get personal again. In mid-August 2008, two months after my strange meetings in the abandoned London headquarters of RBS—with the man I later believed to be Fred Goodwin, in his expensive blue suit, smiling cautiously and observing my reactions to his questions—RBS sent three of its bankers to my office in London, who demanded an $85 million margin call in cash. I was, at the time, a billionaire but, even for a billionaire, $85 million is a lot of cash to come up with in one morning. When I tried to explain that to them, they immediately resorted to threats.

'We'll provoke default!'

It was a Yakuza (Japanese gangster) type stand-off, as I later told my daughter Airi, when she saw how scared I was in that meeting.

'Bankers sometimes behave like Yakuza, they wanted me to cut off my finger as a form of submission. I offered them tea instead.'

She laughed. At the time, I was tempted to pull out, close the RBS account, and trade OTC again, without the hassle of these increasingly bizarre and outrageous margin calls, but I had long positions and ongoing FFAs that were worth seeing through. So there was a Yakuza stand-off between RBS and TMT for a while, as I tried to figure out how to pay the banksters without damaging any other parts of my business.

Eventually I figured that, if I couldn't use cash, I could at least suggest something of equal value to them, so I offered shares instead. I was a major stockholder in a company called Vantage Drilling, an offshore company that specialized in ultra-deepwater drilling, capable of reaching depths in excess of 10,000 feet. I proposed that I could give them 12.1 million shares in Vantage Drilling, which had a market value of $85 million at that time. They smiled broadly. I remember one of them, a Greek bankster called Andy Georgiou, his face went from furious to friendly in a matter of seconds. What I didn't know then, even though TMT owned shares in Vantage, their main banker was JPMorgan Chase. He'd been able to carry out the orders of his boss, Fred Goodwin.

I didn't know it at the time, but I was doing exactly what they wanted—which explained why Georgiou's smile was so wide. Fred Goodwin must have cheered when they gave him the news that I was playing their game. Shares, unlike cash, can fluctuate in value. Who could say that 12.1 million shares in Vantage Drilling would be worth the same next week as they were this week? So, to use them as collateral for FFA trading, someone at RBS would have to value them and make sure they were still worth what I said they were worth. This valuation gave RBS an opportunity to, once again, bend the figures to suit their will. In hindsight, it might've been easier for everybody if I'd just written them a blank check.

The same day that they demanded the $85 million, an RBS general counsel lawyer called Alex Boucher emailed me from New York via the offices of the law firm Allen & Overy, with copies going to Vantage Drilling's general counsel, Chris Celano, in Houston, Texas. These emails discussed how it would be possible to make a short pledge document (a pledged asset is transferred to a lender for the purpose of securing debt) for the Vantage shares I was hoping to use. This short pledge document was signed by the Continental Stock Exchange in New York and another document was drawn up by Ince & Co (my lawyers at the time), and Vantage, as an agreement between Vantage and RBS. That should give you some idea of how complicated the procedure was.

These documents were finally ready on August 22 and I signed them and sent them to my lawyers at Ince the same day. That afternoon, the lawyers got back to me and said there'd been a small mistake, so I'd have to sign again. I was busy getting ready to travel for business purposes in my private jet, so I didn't think too much about it and signed the amended documents the next day. I trusted my team of lawyers to pick up on any adverse changes. That was a mistake! Years later, when I realized that my account at RBS had been beset by countless damaging raids, I had a team of investigators look over the two separate documents that I signed. They found that the two sets were far more different than they first appeared. One contract was written up in an Italian font and the other in a French font, implying they were written up separately. Secondly, the first set had a three-day default clause and the second set a one-day default clause, while the banking hours of Taiwan, London, and New York. One was registered with RBS Edinburgh head office and the other with RBS London head office. Later, a lobbyist I hired called Sovereign Strategies, commented that one of the pledge agreements looked strangely similar to a CDO. Could it be possible, I wondered, that they were betting on the value of the shares?

Whatever the case, it's clear that I signed two very different sets of documents, which gave RBS great leeway over what they could do with my shares which aided the plot to destroy TMT. I believe RBS created 85 million shares with one set of the documents I signed, valued at a $100 per share, which gave the bank $8.5 billion. We discovered that, not only did they vastly over-value the shares, but they registered them as TMT shares, even though Today Makes Tomorrow was a private company and, as such, could not own its own shares. The same day that my accounts showed 85 million shares in TMT, RBS debited my account with $85 million and took the cash out the next day without saying a word.

Such a lot of, to put it mildly, discrepancies taking place over such a short period! Around that time RBS also created a small hedge fund subsidiary called Silver Street with a former head of futures at Bear Stearns. The TMT accounts and Silver Street accounts were right next to each other in the database of a country called TW—which obviously meant Taiwan. Perhaps they were purposely set up that way to make what happened next look as though it could've been another innocent example of human or computer error—so many "errors"! While my account at RBS held the falsely inflated, and so-called TMT, shares, the Silver Street account held my real Vantage Drilling shares, worth $85 million. I believe one of the reasons why the real shares were kept in Silver Street is because RBS wanted TMT to default—which would've happened if I wasn't able to come up with the money after only one day, which was the default clause period in the second set of documents.

So, we've now got 85 million fictitious TMT shares worth $8.5 billion in one account, and 12.1 million Vantage shares worth $85 million in another account. An independent accountancy firm made these observations:

VANTAGE SHARES

A pledge agreement dated 22 August 2008 was entered into by and among RBS, F3 Capital and TMT in relation to Pledged Vantage Shares. There appears to be a number of inconsistencies with the pledge agreement, specifically the reference number at the footer of the pages varied between "NEWYORK/.3 3.06.2129.00 321351" and "3.06.2129.00 321351," there was no financing statement attached and pages 10 and 11 are missing from the agreement.

Under the "CONFIRMATIONS" section on the daily statement of 22 August 2008, an entry of 85 million "PHYSICAL TMT SHARES PLEDGE" was lodged. This appears to be related to the Pledged Vantage Shares and the value shown in the "OPEN POSITIONS" section of the daily statement is USD25.5 million.

There is a "TRADING SUMMARY REPORT FOR MARIE CHANG-LONDON" run on 1 October 2008 where an entry of 85 million "VTG PHYSICAL" of UDS100 each was deleted. This appears to be deleting the Pledged Vantage Shares. The broker is shown as "7TMTC" which appears to be indicating TMT is the broker; this appears to be a discrepancy, as TMT is not a broker. It could be calculated that 85 million shares at USD100 each is USD8.5 billion. This looks very extraordinary as I consider the figure of "85,000,000" to be the value of the Pledged Vantage Shares as at 22 August 2008. It shall not be the number of Vantage Shares pledged by TMT/F3 Capital. It is obvious that the nature of this transaction is unclear and warrants further investigation.

On the daily statement of 30 September 2008 (i.e., about 40 days after the Vantage Shares were pledged), the 85 million shares were withdrawn and 12,142,858 "PHYSICAL TMT SHARES PLEDGE" was lodged. It appears that the entry mentioned above was amended and that this transaction in fact relates to the Pledged Vantage Shares. However, it is abnormal that the value of the shares is shown at USD78,685.72. The closing price of Vantage Shares as at 30 September 2008 was USD2.29 per share. The total market value of Pledged Vantage Shares shall be USD36,307,145.

I do not have any clue as to how the value of securities at USD78,695.72 was determined. It appears to me that RBS could give the pledge any value.

This is an incredibly significant event in my overall story and it sounds very complicated, doesn't it? However, I don't want to add any further simplification at this point, as I will be covering it in detail in my next book. For now, suffice it to say that it was part of the plan to destroy Today Makes Tomorrow and cover up the evidence of the banks' Plan B.

The reason they needed TMT to provoke default was so they could shred the evidence of what they did with the false TMT shares—creating the CDS on AIG—which would protect the US banks if Plan A (too big to fail) didn't work out. It was done to provoke default at the end of the third quarter 2008. Somehow, I managed to avoid the default they so desperately wanted by reducing our positions, cutting down and selling our various forward freight agreements, and selling a few huge deals on to my competitor, Polys Haji-Ioannou, and his Troodos Maritime International SA empire. But more on that later.

You might wonder what happened to that CDS? Surely there must be some evidence of it? The appropriate documentation was probably drawn up, but a few years after the financial crash, RBS was smart enough to buy, dismantle, and then sell off a subsidiary called RBS Taiwan. It's really the perfect way to destroy evidence. You create a small company, stuff it full of all the documents you don't want seen, then you dismantle it. Think of it as the financial equivalent of an acid bath. You see, they couldn't just hide the CDS, because that would leave a large hole in the balance sheet. It was too big to hide. So, RBS covered it up by dumping the evidence in a dismantled subsidiary. But Goldman Sachs, who ended up owning it, had another method. In 2012 they moved the CDS to London and traded it. Then they targeted the trader, changing the limit by which he could trade over 300 times and then they had him arrested. The record of the CDS was chalked up to one of his many mistakes.

As we've seen, Plan A depended on Lehman Brothers being allowed not just to go under, but also being deliberately forced under the water, shocking governments around the world into introducing quantitative easing.

Plan B was the large and carefully created CDS which would provide the banks with appropriate compensation should the Federal Reserve refuse to bail out AIG and herald the era of quantitative easing, but it never had to go into action.

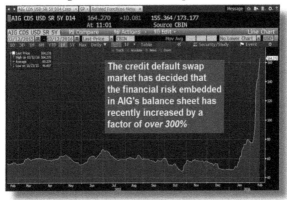

The CDS

THE PARADOX

At the risk of repeating myself by making the point again, I believe Lehman Brothers was sacrificed in order to prove, once and for all, that the banks were now "too big to fail." Plan A was to allow Lehman and Bear Stearns to go under to create a short-term crisis that could be exploited for the bankers' benefit and force Hank Paulson's hand. Lehman had much less exposure than the larger banks like Citigroup, JPMorgan Chase, or Bank of America, yet they were chosen to fail. As their lawyer pointed out during the bankruptcy filing, if TARP had been pushed through before they declared then Lehman would've survived.

It was targeted because it wasn't under the supervision of the SEC, which meant that, unlike the others, they were not obligated to disclose major events and issues. As John Lanchester wrote in London Review of Books, "Bankocracy," after reviewing Joseph Tibman's well-regarded study of the financial collapse from a UK perspective:

> *The most important lesson of Lehman was that it established, irrefutably, the fact that the big Western banks are now Too Big to Fail. Their size, and their interconnectedness, is such that these institutions can't be allowed to die a natural death, whatever happens. These banks have an implicit guarantee that if they ever get sufficiently deeply into trouble, the taxpayers will be there to bail them out.*

Another reason why the bankers might have selected Lehman Brothers as a sacrificial lamb rather than, say, AIG is because if bailout funds had been given to Lehman, it would have stayed within the bank and helped get it back on its feet. Whereas the money that went to AIG then went straight to 14 other central banks to whom the insurance giant owed money, since they were counterparties for its derivative exposures. Why didn't the Fed just give Lehman Brothers enough time to work out a deal with Barclays? A Fed insider told New York Magazine the November after Lehman's collapse that 'they could have found a way to save Lehman.' My question is, why didn't they? I think it was a combination of the plan concocted by top-tier bankers to force it to fail, and Hank Paulson's personal dislike of Dick Fuld. When I met him, years later, I didn't find Fuld to be personable, but he wasn't detestable enough to warrant almost bringing the Western financial system to its knees.

My meeting with Dick Fuld was short. I was in New York and, in the midst of reading about the financial crisis of 2008 and its aftermath, I suddenly recognized the name of the street I was strolling down. It was the same street where Dick Fuld had his new offices.

I thought to myself, 'Why not give it a try?'

It's not every day you find yourself with an opportunity to meet one of the men you've been investigating. I walked into reception.

'I'd like to see Dick Fuld.'

'And you are?'

'I'm Nobu Sue, a former client.'

They called up to Dick Fuld's secretary and, in under ten minutes I found myself sitting across from the infamous CEO in a large, stately office with panoramic views of Manhattan. There was no sign of the stuffed bear!

Without making small talk, I told him I believed he'd been, rightly or wrongly, set up by his fellow bankers. Dick Fuld gave me a long look. I could see the cogs turning behind his dark eyes as he carefully assessed me. He became uneasy when I mentioned Nomura—but he confirmed my Plan B suspicions. It had been, indeed, too big to hide. That was a huge moment in my life; that confirmation was what I'd been looking for during the past eight years. There was a long silence between us, laden with unspoken significance.

Then he stood up.

'Could you leave now, please?'

So I did.

I doubt if I was the first person to tell Dick Fuld he'd been an unwitting scapegoat. As the *Financial Times* noted on September 17, 2008, shortly after its collapse:

> *On Friday 12th September, Lehman Brothers was an investment grade bank with $42 billion of liquid assets. On Monday 15th September, it was bankrupt. Why?*

Many have noted that Lehman wasn't in a substantially worse position than other banks. Was there really no way it could have been kept afloat for just one week, until TARP, the big bailout gift that saved Wall Street, was passed? What's more, the process that Lehman underwent is called uncontrolled bankruptcy, which basically means the regulators took a "let's sit back and see who appears to pick at the corpse" approach. It's the most damaging kind of bankruptcy filing there is. So, when Timothy Geithner, Hank Paulson, and Ben Bernanke looked at the smoldering remains of Lehman Brothers and decided they couldn't let another bank go like that, was there really no alternative but to pump billions and billions into the system? Couldn't they have figured out a way to ease and facilitate the process of filing for bankruptcy in a way that both minimized the negative impact and upheld the ethos of moral hazard? To me, it seems an awful lot like trying to cut down a tree with a steak knife, then declaring all trees impervious to harm and giving up. It wasn't necessarily a bad idea just because, on the first try, they went about it the wrong way.

All of this is a side note to the fact that Lehman's sudden bankruptcy was partly exacerbated by poisonous rumors and short-selling. Rumors led to investors pulling out and short-selling forced prices down. Short-selling isn't, technically, supposed to have such a powerful effect because, if it did, then rival companies could use the technique to destroy their competitors. In short-selling, it's legally required that the person selling the shares will have to buy them back—much like futures, short-selling involves trading with "future" shares. The reason this makes a profit is because you believe the share price will fall. The problem was, a year later, the SEC (not responsible for Lehman) discovered that 32.8 billion Lehman Brothers shares were not repurchased. This is a huge red flag! Of course, every year there's a small percentage of shares that aren't repurchased via short-selling, but 32.8 billion? That's unheard of and a strong indicator of fraud. Yet the SEC have never investigated this, at least not publicly, even though failed trades (an indicator of possible illegal short-selling) made up 23% of Lehman trades in the days preceding its collapse.

If it wasn't for the injurious rumors and trades, if Barclays hadn't pulled out last minute, if the Fed had given them time or aided them through a controlled bankruptcy, then it's likely the aftereffects of Lehman's failure would've been softened and Hank Paulson wouldn't have felt the need to take such extreme and rushed action. He wouldn't have started to pour billions into Wall Street with the desperation of a lone man throwing buckets of water on a forest fire.

In no way am I saying that Lehman Brothers was innocent or worthy of our sympathy. They intentionally falsified their balance sheets (using an accounting trick known as Repo 105), they turned down Korea Development Bank's offer and embodied every single predictable, boorish, testosterone-fueled trope on Wall Street. The only reason they were so successful prior to the crises is because of their leverage policy of 30:1, which, believe it or not, meant that for every dollar they had, they had 30 dollars of debt. It's not because I've got any regard in my heart for Lehman Brothers that I began to wonder whether they were intentionally sacrificed, but because, if they were, it meant that private individuals and corporations forced the US government and the Federal Reserve Bank into a corner, so they'd have to hand over the money. It was a stick-up! It was a long and complicated form of entrapment. Lehman was pushed to the brink and almost took the US economy with it, so the point could be proved that no bank could ever be allowed to fail again.

It worked!

We now live in a world with publicly funded private corporations. We live in a world where the taxpayer takes on the risk that makes the bankers rich, but gets none of the profit. Every industry can say their success enriches the whole of society, but the financial industry is the only one that can hold us all hostage. Dick Fuld might have been the prime patsy, but there's no doubt in my mind that we were all victims of the scam.

On September 12 Ben Bernanke and Timothy Geithner called a "hands-on-deck" meeting in New York. No representative of Lehman Brothers was present, but all their competitors were—JPMorgan Chase, Citigroup, Credit Suisse, Merrill Lynch, Morgan Stanley, Hank Paulson's old firm, Goldman Sachs, and the chairlady of Citizens Financial Group, a wholly owned subsidiary of RBS. There are no comprehensive records of what went on in that room and the meeting has become the focal point of huge speculation. It was, without a doubt, a pivotal moment in financial history that will remain forever clouded in mystery. The fact that no one has spoken about it either shows they know their actions wouldn't be interpreted favorably, or perhaps they were asked to sign non-disclosure agreements—not an uncommon practice in the boardrooms of high finance. Whatever went down in that room, after the meeting it was agreed that Lehman Brothers would get no help from anyone.

Goldman Sachs oversaw the destruction of their biggest competitor, with the sanction and approval of the Federal Reserve. They did this in the same way the USA and UK were shouldered into going to war with Iraq—by utilizing a large and terrifying threat. The threat of a second and bigger Lehman Brothers was the Weapon of Mass Destruction that mobilized Congress into funneling billions of taxpayer dollars into Wall Street.

The meeting on September 12 occurred in the evening, with the CEOs of the various banks arriving around 6:00pm, along with representatives from Deutsche Bank, Royal Bank of Scotland, and BNP Paribas. The New York Federal Reserve Bank looks like a prison disguised as a Renaissance palace, with turrets, lanterns, window grilles, and an underground vault that contains the largest stockpile of gold in the world. Officially, during the meeting Hank Paulson asked these banks to put aside their rivalry and unite to purchase Lehman's less palatable assets, the toxic ones no prospective buyer would want. Unofficially, Geithner then divided the bankers into three groups to problem-solve various options and solutions. They valued Lehman's troubled assets, considered ways of selling Lehman Brothers, and prepared for its bankruptcy. The irony of the exercise was, nobody really cared about Lehman.

By the next day the only useful proposition they'd come up with was a request for the Fed to establish a line of credit support to "other banks" who were in danger of ending up like Lehman Brothers—that is, themselves!

By the end of September 13, a bank had been saved, but it wasn't Lehman Brothers—it was Merrill Lynch. Merrill was purchased by Bank of America, who, up until then, had displayed a strong interest in buying Lehman. It purchased Merrill Lynch for $50 billion. By the end of the day the general counsel for the New York Fed called Lehman and told them to file for bankruptcy by midnight, so the markets would have time to recover, slightly, from the shock before Monday morning. No one at Lehman Brothers understood how this could have happened. How could a room full of intelligent men, with more power at their disposal than ever before, have failed to get them an extension or a buyer? Well, the answer is simple—they didn't want to! The civil servants wanted Lehman Brothers to fail because the US government wished to uphold its principle that the free market would right itself, that moral hazard was paramount, and it was listening to a populace who didn't want their tax dollars going to Wall

Street. The CEOs and bankers wanted Lehman Brothers to fail because they were a rival and they wanted to prove to the US government and the Federal Reserve that allowing a bank to fail caused destruction, pain, and volatility. They wanted to put an end to the argument for moral hazard.

It was a paradox.

The bankers won!

Hank Paulson—US Treasury Secretary

Jamie Dimon—CEO of JPMorgan Chase

COLUMBUS DAY GIFT

In September 2008: Fannie Mae and Freddie Mac, government-sponsored enterprises, went down; Lehman Brothers went down; HBOS, a centuries-old Scottish bank and major rival to Royal Bank of Scotland, went down and was purchased by Lloyds; Merrill Lynch was purchased by Bank of America; AIG was nationalized in all but name; two smaller American banks, Washington Mutual and Wachovia, also failed. Ireland, shortly followed by Greece, shocked the world by underwriting its entire banking system and promising to support it at any cost.

The controlled crisis had finally reached its peak. The markets were tumbling into disarray and US officials were beginning to worry less about the moral implications of propping up the investment banks and more about falling into a prolonged, L-shaped (most severe) recession, like the one Japan was still struggling to recover from. Everyone agreed, from the economics departments of top universities to the corridors of the White House, in the boardrooms of investment banks and at the news desks of network television, that the markets reacted well to good news and bad news, but went into meltdown over uncertainty. The mood changed in mid-September and the goal became to act swiftly and decisively. The time for second-guessing was over!

The banks were almost there. Governments all over the world were beginning to seriously consider recapitalizing them. They'd pushed the planet to the brink and were now about to receive their ransom—and I'm not using the word ransom lightly. RBS called Alistair Darling, the Chancellor of the Exchequer in the UK, and told him that if they weren't bailed out that day, then they'd go down and take the British economy with them. Hank Paulson, when he attempted to pass a bailout bill in mid-September, told Congress that, unless they gave him what he wanted, then $5.5 trillion would be sliced from the GDP that afternoon and the world economy would collapse. At every turn, our politicians, journalists, and civil servants were unable to make considered, well-informed decisions because they were being harangued and bullied into giving the banks what they were demanding so urgently.

And the little they requested in return, that the banks should use the bailout funds to increase lending to the public or, at the very least, record how and when they spent the money, wasn't met. The US Treasury was told that those meagre requirements would stop institutions from accepting the money. The government was attempting to inject liquidity into 500 banks, including those that didn't necessarily want it, because they believed the system needed more money to start trading properly again. Somehow, even though they were the ones that caused the crisis and desperately needed the cash, the big banks had the upper hand. They could negotiate any terms they wanted because, if the bailout wasn't favorable enough, they could threaten to self-implode and the government wasn't sure if it could risk calling their bluff. The banks were in complete control.

No lending requirement was ever made of them.

In fact, since the financial crisis, many of them, including JPMorgan Chase's Jamie Dimon, have acted as if they did the taxpayer a favor by taking the money.

Dimon is quoted as saying to the Senate Banking, Housing and Urban Affairs Committee in June 2012 that they only took the money 'because we were asked to by the Treasury Secretary.'

This is as truculently ungrateful and arrogant as it sounds. Over and over again, JPMorgan Chase and Goldman Sachs have reiterated the lie that they didn't need the bailout money and only took it because they'd been told by US officials that they had to, for the benefit of the overall economy. I find that hard to believe since, only a couple of weeks before, these "healthy" banks, in no need of rescue, had refused to lend to, or aid, Lehman Brothers, with the excuse that they were struggling themselves and not able to.

The banks were succeeding in their plan to receive huge amounts of funding with no strings attached. However, one "problem" might have thrown a spanner in the works.

While the White House was trying to push through the Troubled Asset Relief Program, a presidential election was underway. The Republican candidate (John McCain) and the Democratic candidate (Barack Obama) were battling it out to see who would replace George W Bush in the White House, and John McCain suspended campaigning to return to Washington and join the effort to save the financial system. This sounds like a man doing his political duty, but it also meant that "the crisis," which was deepening, was now becoming an electioneering tactic.

Neither campaign was in full support of TARP. It was in their best interests to denounce any policies that might infuriate the electorate. Left-wing voters didn't like the idea of bailing out the rich, and right-wing voters didn't like "big government" getting involved in private business. Congress was making it difficult for the bankers to get their big pay-off. The entire process was rushed, jumbled, and confused. Hank Paulson was accused by one of his own men of over-simplifying the process to the point of absurdity. The toxic assets that TARP was asserting the government should buy up, in exchange for the bailout, were, in truth, so complex it would take weeks, and maybe months, to establish their true value.

By September 27 the US Treasury was becoming increasingly desperate as Congress failed to reach a compromise. They tried to impress on the politicians the severity of the crisis and attempted a new tactic, summed up by Neel Kashkari, Assistant Secretary at the US Treasury.

'We've got to scare the shit out of them!'

In real terms, they started to use the same tactics the banksters had used against them. They stopped talking about the specifics of the proposed legislation and started to reiterate the extent of the potential recession they were facing. Washington Mutual (a savings bank) had just collapsed and been purchased by JPMorgan Chase. Wachovia (the fourth largest bank holding company in the USA) was also wobbling. Both political parties were holding out until they could get proper oversight for the program: a reduction of bonuses; proof that buying toxic assets was preferable to simply giving the banks money; and the possibility of paying out in instalments rather than in one giant lump sum. But Hank Paulson wasn't giving them a straight answer. The truth was, the markets had been brought to the brink of collapse and the fear of causing more confusion was leading to rash solutions that simply weren't convincing.

Personally, I find it surprising that neither the Democrats nor the Republicans managed to convince Hank Paulson to put a cap on bonuses in return for the bailout funds. They knew how politically damaging it would be for the banksters who'd caused the crash to personally benefit from taxpayers' money. However, Paulson managed to convince them that installing the condition of a cap on bonuses would prevent firms from accessing the cash, just like the banks had convinced him that his accountability measures would do the same. The excuse was, it would take too long to renegotiate contracts. I disagree. If the financial crisis has shown us anything, it's that if there's a will, there's a way. If the US government managed to raise and free-up trillions of dollars to pour into the banks on such short notice—if they managed to prevent a larger global downturn that could have lasted decades—then I'm sure they could have found a solution to the tricksy legislative problem of bonuses.

I believe the will simply wasn't there.

Hank Paulson, as an ex-Goldman Sachs man, had been on the receiving end of such bonuses for most of his adult life. He was too much a part of the system to see it function in any other way and that was another great flaw in his plan. Hank Paulson, as pure as his motivations were, wanted the financial sector to return to the status quo. An opportunity to truly heal the problems that led to the crisis was missed. I don't know if this was due to a lack of imagination or vested interests but I do know that, because the causes weren't fixed, we'll be seeing another crisis one day—maybe very soon. In fact (as Adam McKay warned in The Big Short), investment banks are now trading a bond called a Bespoke Tranche Opportunity—which is just financial engineering speak for a synthetic CDO!

At the time I wasn't the only one with strong reservations. The first time Hank Paulson attempted to get TARP through Congress, on September 29, 2008, it was rejected by 228 votes to 205. The Republicans were strongly opposed out of a fear it would lead to the nationalization of the financial sector—and some of the more left-leaning Democrats were also opposed. As a reaction, the Dow Jones experienced its largest point loss in a single day. However, I don't think this worried the banksters at all. They knew the government would have to bail them out. How and when that happened was Hank Paulson's and Timothy Geithner's job, not theirs.

On October 3 TARP went to the vote once more. It was expanded from three pages to 450 and the final product was a strange document that even included sweeteners such as tax breaks for the manufacturers of children's wooden arrows—to try to win over the more truculent members of the House. I think it's safe to say that a great deal of lobbying went into the final draft. It's a common but questionable practice in politics to offer your opponents a favor, or maybe we should just call it a bribe, in return for their vote. That's not to say that some of the last-minute additions weren't commendable—like the $8 billion in tax relief on college tuition fees for those who had suffered losses in the natural disasters that occurred in the Midwest and Gulf Coast, or for companies that produced and used renewable fuel. It included billions of dollars in funding for rural schools and tax relief on the settlements received by those affected by the Exxon Valdez oil spill. The consensus seems to have been that, if the US Treasury was going to bail out the banks, then it should help others too.

However, when TARP was finally passed and $700 billion was earmarked for its deployment, the Treasury was still working out its main components and questioning whether they should spend all of it buying up toxic assets after all. They called up Wall Street bankers again and asked for their "impartial" advice. Warren Buffett (Berkshire Hathaway holding company) suggested a complex but well thought through plan, in which the government would set up a publicly owned, semi-private firm to manage the toxic assets. But the overwhelming advice from Wall Street was that they should invest directly in financial institutions in return for preferred stock (priority over common stock), which would mean that when (if) the markets recovered, the taxpayer would make a return on their investment.

When the British government announced that it was investing £87 billion in eight national banks—including the terminally ill Royal Bank of Scotland, who were still playing fast and loose with my money—that sealed Hank Paulson's resolve. I suspect he didn't want to be the last man standing at the upcoming G7 summit, set to happen on Columbus Day weekend (October 11–13). Every European country was starting to get its act together. The scheme—the controlled crisis—had worked everywhere! Only America was left, dragging its heels as it clung onto long-held, libertarian, free-market ideologies that, frankly, no longer had any place in a hyper-connected, turbo-capitalistic, global economy.

But, unlike the British government, Hank Paulson didn't want to lend just to the banks that desperately needed to be bailed out, he thought he could trick the market by lending to every bank that qualified, whether they needed the funds or not. His logic for this decision was, if the Treasury used

TARP to fund every bank, then investors would have no way of knowing which banks had been in serious trouble and which hadn't. His fear was, if they only bailed out the banks that needed it, investors would be wary, their stock would plummet, and they'd hemorrhage more money than the Treasury was pouring in. He didn't want the market to turn against those banks just because they were receiving funds from the Treasury. Of course, it's hard to trick the market and there are far more indicators as to the health of an organization than whether or not they've accepted a government bailout.

Who knows if it worked? We only have one version of history, but I do think the money would've been better spent if it had been allocated according to need and not out of some hare-brained attempt to trick investors—and maybe they might not have had to provide additional bailouts later on. I even wonder if Hank Paulson's desire to dupe investors into treating solvent and insolvent banks equally isn't, in itself, morally dubious.

Another consequence of wanting to distribute funds to all the major banks was that Hank Paulson had now put himself in a situation where he had to convince the boards and CEOs of nine major financial institutions to take the money. If those banks didn't have to take the cash because they were viable, healthy, and solvent (as healthy as you can be during a financial crash) then he could hardly include the sorts of caveats, restrictions, and regulations that many in the White House and most of the public wanted. But, as I said, G7 was coming up. Paulson's reputation, and by extension the reputation of the United States of America, was on the line. He invited a group of CEOs from Wall Street to Washington for an urgent meeting. Apparently they weren't told what the meeting was about, only that it would make them happy. This group would forever be known as the "Big 9."

Paulson sat them down and told them: 'To encourage wide participation, the program is designed to provide an attractive source of capital, on identical terms, to all qualifying financial institutions. We will state clearly that you are healthy institutions, participating in order to support the US economy.'

To hear his rhetoric you'd think Wall Street's Big 9 were setting themselves up as heroes, when in fact they were about to be on the receiving end of huge cash injections of public money. Bank of America, Citigroup, JPMorgan Chase and Wells Fargo (who would acquire Wachovia in December 2008 in a government-forced sale) were to get $25 billion each. Goldman Sachs, Morgan Stanley and State Street (an asset management company) were to receive $10 billion apiece.

There it was, a big Columbus Day gift. They all signed on the dotted line and Hank Paulson could finally catch up on some sorely needed sleep. According to the US government the economy had just been saved. It wasn't for a couple of years, as the public watched banksters continue to pay themselves huge bonuses and make irrational and dangerous trades, that anyone started to question whether we should have bailed them out, or how exactly the bailout was handled. At the time, the banks had successfully pushed us to the brink and every civil servant in the world was scrambling to pull us back the only way they knew how.

Money poured into Wall Street at the expense of the general public, and I'm not saying the people who pulled it off did so out of any underlying disposition towards malice or evil. No, they simply had an innate sense of vested interest and could value the significance of a collapsing bank more than the significance of a 100,000 lost jobs across all sectors. Also, the rhetoric of the financial industry is bombastic. They tell us over and over again that their industry is the most important, the most powerful, the greatest contributor to the economy as a whole. They say they're the ones who provide loans to small businesses, to home owners, to auto buyers, to all of us. They remind us that, without them, we would be nothing. In answer I'd like to quote Paul Volcker, former chairman of the Federal Reserve:

'I wish that somebody would give me some shred of neutral evidence about the relationship between financial innovation recently and the growth of the economy, just one shred of information. The most important financial innovation that I have seen over the years is the automatic teller machine. That really helps people.'

The truth is, the banks left their traditional role behind years ago and now a great deal of what they do just isn't all that useful or central to the global economy. What's more, a lot of those banks who so "reluctantly" took the bailout funds, who had to be wooed into receiving financial aid, then had to ask for more money just over a year later. By 2009 Citigroup had received $45 billion in total, and 36% of it was owned by American taxpayers. Bank of America requested another $20 billion. I think this proves that their reluctance was just another game of brinkmanship so they could get the liquidity they so desperately needed, consequence-free. I'm sure they all learned how to do it in the boardrooms of their respective firms. If you're making a deal, don't let the counterparty know how much you want it. Bluff. Isn't bluffing one of the great tricks of the gambler? And Wall Street is full of gamblers.

So, we've reached the part in the financial crisis when the New York Federal Reserve opened up all their various discount windows and money-lending schemes to the credit-thirsty banks. September 2008 has been and gone. Lehman Brothers is bust. AIG has been rescued with a huge bailout, thanks to the obscure law called Section 13 (3), even though it's a non-bank and outside the Fed's jurisdiction. TARP, the Troubled Asset Relief Program, has been passed by a reluctant Congress and $700 billion has been made available to the banksters. Moral hazard is over and quantitative easing is here to stay. The banks have managed to prove, once and for all that, with a little help from the mining and shipping industries, they are "too big to fail".

If the US Treasury had realized how desperately the banks needed their support, if they'd done due diligence and properly checked the balance sheets and not, as is a recurring theme in this story, asked other banks to do it for them, maybe they'd have also realized they were in a stronger negotiating position than they thought. They could have requested the curb on bonuses that Congress wanted. They could have put in stipulations that required the banks to use a certain percentage of the funds for small loans to the public. They could have included stricter limits on leverage-to-equity ratio. They could have stopped investment banks from incentivizing risk. They could have created stronger and more independent regulators. They could have implemented new rules to prevent the clever tricks banks use to obscure their balance sheets. Simply put, they had had an opportunity to really improve the financial sector and therefore prevent a similar crash from occurring again.

I suppose that's what we forget when we remember the crisis, that it was preventable. The bankers forget it too when they complain, yet again, that everybody hates them, that they're the unfair scapegoats, easy targets for politicians, subject to vitriolic attacks from every corner, and with nothing to console them but their net worth. They forget that this crash was caused by their industry. They forget that, had they not pushed for deregulation in the 1980s, the crash would never have happened. They flourished from the benefits of deregulation, but were unprepared to accept the blame when it got out of hand. I can't help but wonder whether their arrogance and disdain for all non-bankers isn't why there's still so much anger directed against them.

Then again, I also understand that arrogance. After all, they pulled off what was arguably the largest scam in human history. They got Hank Paulson and Timothy Geithner to give them shitloads of taxpayer money and, what's more, they got them to beg the banks to take it.

But if committing the crime was easy, getting away with it—that's the hard part!

US Congress

THE LAKATAMIA DEAL

In 2017 the news broke that John Varley, the CEO of Barclays during the tumultuous time of the financial crash, was to face criminal charges for fraud. The man who, with Bob Diamond, oversaw Barclays at the time when they duped Lehman Brothers into believing they were their one and only savior, before pulling out at the last minute. Whereas Bob Diamond, a figure who historically has taken the brunt of the criticism because he was the man in New York facilitating it, and apparently the man who wanted it to happen, is completely absent from the case. John Varley was indicted because Barclays raised money from Qatari investors, including a Qatari sovereign fund, in June and October 2008. They managed to raise £11.8 billion but it has since come to light that the money came with various side deals attached, which included a £322 million payment made by Barclays to Qatar, and a $3 billion loan from Barclays to the Qatari national bank. Why loan Qatar Holdings (a subsidiary of Qatar Investment Authority, Qatar's state-owned holding company) billions of dollars when you're in need of a loan yourself? According to an advisor called upon as a witness in court, this loan was used by Qatar Holdings to fund its investment in Barclays shares, which means that Barclays was lending to itself.

That is serious fraud!

These sums are huge and clear indicators that something was definitely going on beneath the surface. Yet it still took the Serious Fraud Office (SFO) five years of investigation before they felt they could press charges.

These financial regulatory bodies simply don't like prosecuting big banks, or maybe they don't have the manpower or know-how to get past the tricks and dodgy legalities that are second nature to massive corporations? I'm glad John Varley and his cohorts were brought to book for their fraudulent actions, which seem to include similar crimes to those I suspect Royal Bank of Scotland have committed; specifically, conspiracy to commit fraud by false representation, when they told their investors they were strong and stable to trick them into buying more shares and raising money during the rights issue. Also, there are similarities between Barclays lending to itself via Qatar Holdings and RBS/JPMorgan Chase lending to themselves via the PDCF. This case reaffirmed my belief that the corporate decisions I believe RBS and others were guilty of, are neither out of the ordinary nor would be considered particularly immoral by the banksters themselves. They seem to have an inherent character trait that allows them to conduct business, conscience-free, without any consideration or respect for the law. It's often easier to plead guilty, pay a fine, and avoid criminal charges rather than spend a single day in court. If banks aren't made to pay dearly for fraudulent activities like lending to themselves, then there's nothing to stop them from doing it again, and again, and again.

A few people at Barclays piped up, saying the alleged fraud was "victimless" and that, more importantly, it saved Barclays from having to accept the taxpayer-funded bailout. But I think they're missing the point—which is, if banks can just lend to themselves whenever they're in financial distress then they undermine the most basic principles of money. If they can print, endlessly, any amount of cash they need, then it destroys the value of that money. Money is just a cipher—its underlying value comes from the resources it is exchanged for, be it mined diamonds or an hour of your labor. If they aren't exchanging anything for their money, then it becomes valueless—nothing—useless. And the system that produces it is corrupt. It's a perfect example of the kind of elitist injustice that large corporations utilize. Imagine what would happen if their average mortgage recipient tried the same trick—there'd certainly be jail time involved.

The major banks would have done anything to survive during the crash and believed they were perfectly justified in doing so. To them, I and countless others like me were just plebeians who were stupid enough to be taken for a ride. A con man never feels sympathy for his mark—if you're stupid enough to fall for the con, then you deserve to be cheated.

But Barclays made a mistake using a Qatari sovereign bank to loan themselves money. Qatar is a small nation with the third-highest oil reserves in the world and the highest per capita income. Their royal family owns the global media group Al Jazeera, a popular and critically acclaimed news outlet that has taken on much bigger fish than Barclays—and won. Yes, the Qatari Holding Bank had the financial clout to give Barclays what they wanted in one fell swoop but it meant that, unlike RBS and perhaps others, Barclays couldn't hide the evidence. I believe they counted on the assumption that the SFO, the Financial Conduct Authority (FCA) and other regulatory bodies were traditionally more bark than bite and that, even if they did file charges, which was probably seen as unlikely, Barclays would just pay the fine like they always did. They decided to wait and see if the regulators would have the gumption to investigate them. Their gamble didn't pay off on this occasion.

The Royal Bank of Scotland had no inclination to wait and see what aspects of their fraud might come to light. They were in a much worse financial position than Barclays, largely due to the acquisition of ABN AMRO—as you know, Barclays also attempted to buy that company, but lost in the auction, which makes you realize that Barclays didn't survive the financial crash in better shape than RBS because of any inherent caution or sense of responsibility, but because they lost out on a major deal. RBS didn't have the Qataris to worry about either—no, the only shred of evidence standing in their way was my company, Today Makes Tomorrow, and a handful of other small businesses.

As I've mentioned before, there was a tried and tested method of destroying individual and company accounts. JPMorgan Chase's sudden demands on Lehman Brothers are often cited as the final shove that tipped Lehman over the edge—and William D. Cohan's piece in the *New York Times* on February 16, 2011, "How Goldman Killed AIG" is an enlightening read. It details how, on July 27, 2007, Goldman Sachs sent a $1.81 billion collateral call to AIG Financial Products to make up for what Goldman (pretty much alone at that point) thought represented the decline in the value of the securities. It was a margin call of unheard of proportions, arriving without notice. It was a margin call that the CEO of AIG Financial Products immediately suspected of being fraudulent. AIG had enough clout to dispute it and refused to pay until Goldman Sachs whittled it down to $600 million. The fact that they were willing to reduce it by over $1 billion when confronted, proves that the original margin call was nothing more than numbers plucked, wishfully, out of the air. However, that didn't stop them from trying the same trick again in September 2007 and AIG finally caved, much against their best interests since, when markets improved and they tried to get some of their money back, Goldman Sachs went suspiciously silent.

The official report compiled by the Financial Crisis Inquiry Committee (FCIC) was published in 2011, after a two-year investigation. You can buy it on Amazon for ten dollars but, at 600 pages written by financiers and politicians, it's not a page-turner. I struggled through it myself, curious to see the official account of a time I'd barely survived. I expected it to be intellectually intriguing, in a dry sort of way, as if I was reading a book about the various trade agreements of the Meiji era. I certainly wasn't expecting the shock of seeing, on the pages in front of me, that the same inconsistencies, and mistakes, and "human errors" that had contributed to the destruction of my business were the very same used to bring down some of the world's largest financial institutions.

I realized, to my disgust and rage, that I'd been taken for a fool and, from that moment on, I made it my life's mission to expose the truth about how TMT was destroyed.

A lot of companies fell during the financial crisis. TMT is just one of the horror stories that keep entrepreneurs awake at night. In the shipping industry we don't refer to 2008 as a crisis or a recession, as if it was a brief and hermetically sealed point in history. No, we still call it the Great Recession. We are one of the few sectors that hasn't fully recovered and, while that's partly down to the financial crisis of 2008 and the sudden withdrawal of credit and loans from banks, it is also the result of more predictable global trends, like the general slowing of China's industrial boom. While they were building their infrastructure, there were more ships on the high seas than ever before—shipping coal and iron ore to make steel beams and tower blocks. But now the demand is slowing and there have already been five bankruptcy filings among the major carriers. As you might imagine, a lot of my friends in the industry can't quite understand why I'm taking the failure of TMT so personally. They don't understand why I won't cease my tireless research and lawsuits and just accept defeat. They want me to move on. They believe Today Makes Tomorrow was just like the other companies that went to the wall during the crash and that I can't accept my own failure.

They could be right.

But I don't think so!

Today Makes Tomorrow shouldn't have failed. We were, in comparison to other companies, well set up to endure whatever market turbulence was heading our way. Historically we had been a frugal company. I purchased secondhand ships, all too wary of shipping's repetitive trend of building too many vessels in times of economic boom and finding itself out on a limb when the bust came along. Even taking account of the huge margin calls, TMT should have survived. When RBS attempted to bankrupt me, I sold off our positions and put up my own personal shares in Vantage Drilling as collateral. Every day I was reducing our exposure to Royal Bank of Scotland's sticky fingers but, unfortunately, I wasn't quick enough.

In July 2008, one month after my meeting with the man I believed to be Fred Goodwin—the man who grilled me for hours and ascertained with a cold smile that I wasn't going to be any trouble—there was another huge margin call on TMT. As already explained, in July 2008 RBS were in the process of using my money to write the CDS on AIG's portfolio and sell it on, eventually, to Goldman Sachs. Meanwhile, the price of iron ore had risen 90% and oil prices reached record highs—pushed up in part, I believe, by speculators at Goldman Sachs. The various margin calls and general volatility left TMT shorter of liquidity than I'd hoped, so I organized a simple trade deal with another shipping company called Lakatamia, operated by a man called Polys Haj-Ioannou.

Polys Haji-Ioannou is a billionaire shipping magnate whose brother, Stelios Haji-Ioannou, founded the stratospherically successful EasyJet. As with my family, the Haji-Ioannous first entered the shipping trade in the 1950s, with nothing but a small loan and an iron will, and grew to be one of its greatest businesses. By all rights we should be the best of friends but, unfortunately, it didn't work out that way.

The deal I struck with Lakatamia was, at its heart, a simple loan but, in true financial fashion, it looks much, much more complicated on paper. Basically, TMT Liberia (the subsidiary I used to trade forward freight agreements) had 7.2 million metric tons worth of future positions in 2009 and Lakatamia agreed to purchase those positions on the basis that I bought them back in a month (August 8, 2008) at a 1% higher rate—so Polys would make 1% of the total contract value. Now, the reason Lakatamia were prepared to take on a deal of this nature was because, firstly, they believed the price of the positions wasn't going to rise and lose them money. Secondly, they told me they wanted to provide the short-term loan on the understanding that I would repay the favor if required to do so. At the time, TMT was a larger and more influential shipping company and people tended to believe I had a good idea of which up-and-coming trades were going to go well and which weren't. The business world relies a lot more on favors and honor than you might think. So, I supposed Lakatamia might be looking for advice in the future. No problem.

The deal in question was "TD3 600MT CAL09 per month." I know, shipping has its own foreign language. Let me break it down for you:

• MT stands for metric tons, so I was propositioning Lakatamia with a future in chartering enough ships to carry 600,000 metric tons of oil per month

• CAL09 means that the shipping was to occur in 2009

• TD3 is a trade route that runs from the Arabian Gulf to Japan, across the Strait of Malacca. It goes through the narrow stretch of water between Iran and the United Arab Emirates, past Pakistan, India, Sri Lanka, between Indonesia and Australia, before coming up past the Philippines to Japan.

When you think of a very large crude carrier (VLCC) slowly making its way past 15 different countries over the course of months, you realize how big the world is. That's what I love most about shipping—when I get the chance to sit back and think about it—it has a reality, a physical and timely consequence to its actions that our communications networks don't. The laptop on my desk and the phone in my pocket shrink the world and make it accessible to me whenever I wish, but the ships edging their way across the vast waters of the world make me realize the true size and majesty of the planet. Of course, you don't get many traders who think like that. Most of the ones I've met couldn't tell you exactly where the TD3 goes, unless there's an outbreak of piracy—they're only interested in the numbers and profits, not the reality. For me, it was always more about the ships than anything else. That's part of the reason why what happened with Lakatamia stung so much.

Polys and I didn't facilitate this idea by ourselves. In fact the whole trade wasn't really our idea at all, but was the "helpful" suggestion of one of Clarksons' traders, who I'd grown accustomed to doing business with. I think I've mentioned that Clarksons is one of the UK's largest shipbroking services. They're based in London but have 36 offices all over the world. They're generally a well-liked and trusted company, having been on the scene since 1852—which is much longer than either Polys or I have been. Shipbrokers are the middlemen of the shipping industry. They organize and smooth trades between shipowners (i.e., TMT) and ship charterers (whoever wants me to carry their goods).

I was grateful, this deal was going to allow me to manage RBS' mad margin call. But there was some suspicious behavior around the Lakatamia deal that had me thinking that perhaps it wasn't the great favor I thought it was. Both TMT and Lakatamia had FFA trading relations with RBS, and it turned out that Lakatamia were a clearing client of RBS, which means they were preapproved and trustworthy, it also meant that RBS knew about TMT's various positions when the TD3 600MT CAL09 trade was proposed and they decided to muscle in on the deal I was doing with Polys (I believe now it was all prearranged).

At the time this was significant because, when they later froze TMT's accounts and refused to let us trade, they claimed not to know that there were any ongoing deals large enough to warrant notice. When I asked an ex-RBS employee why they would allow the trade to pass through their books, albeit briefly, before passing it on to Lakatamia, if they believed I didn't have the appropriate collateral, the answer was, 'I cannot be sure why they did this and see no reason for them doing so, other than for their benefit and to front-run TMT's positions.'

Front-running is a form of insider trading, knowing about a trade in advance and using that knowledge to your personal advantage. It's highly illegal! He told me it was the only reason why RBS would have shouldered their way into a trade that could easily have been done without them as middlemen.

Of course RBS would have benefitted from knowing about this trade. They would have known that, since the trade was capable of shifting the market, they could buy or sell their own positions based on that knowledge. In other words, they could front-run this trade, as they'd been doing with many of my trades, with impunity. Also, they never mentioned to me in any correspondence that RBS would be holding the position, even for a short period—that alone is suspicious. I think RBS realized that, once this position had been sold, it would both reduce their exposure and put TMT in a very vulnerable position, so they didn't want me to buy it back.

RBS reckoned they could front-run this and took the position on July 7, 2008. They held the position, but couldn't front-run it to other parties and needed to work with Polys Haji-Ioannou a month later when they refused to allow me to buy back my position and created the case for a worldwide freezing order, without showing any evidence to the court. RBS froze my accounts, without justification, halfway through the deal, which Lakatamia subsequently used to sue me in 2011.

Polys and RBS colluded with each other to try to solve RBS' losses as the market started to head south at the end of August 2008. RBS asked Polys for a favor—to sell 80% of its position notated to RBS Sempra Commodities without letting TMT know about it for years. RBS did it when TMT had a valuation of $3.6 billion on its books at the end of October (Madoff again). It happened during the American presidential voting week. The bank couldn't receive any money from New York Federal Reserve when it had a legitimate contract to show. So RBS requested Polys to finance personally the entire loss of $92 million—then Polys and RBS had to find a way to claim from TMT.

Three years later, at the trial, Polys Haj-Ioannou lied in court and disclosed documents that showed conflicting accounts of what had happened. Back in 2008 it was a win-win situation for him—he didn't have to trade through RBS—if the market went up he still made his 1%; if it went down he could short-sell and claim TMT's profits. This case is still a mystery, but Polys was personally questioned by KPMG (as auditors) about potential money laundering in 2009. RBS' and Polys' email exchanges and records were not disclosed in the Lakatamia case, which an English judge questioned the quality of.

Again, this is a highly complex event that I'll clarify in my next book. The reason for this is because the story created by Lakatamia wasn't true—they didn't disclose any of the emails between RBS, Polys Haji-Ioannou, and his Troodos Maritime International in Monaco. Neither were the broker's emails on how the positions were traded disclosed, nor how the entities were sold to different companies related to JPMorgan Chase's and RBS Sempra Commodities. If the reader, for now, could just consider it part of the conspiracy to put Today Makes Tomorrow out of business, so the banks could destroy the evidence of the AIG CDS and Plan B.

Polys Haji-Ioannou—a shrewd oil trader and experienced FFA trader

CONSPIRACY

My aim is to discover, through a forensic assessment of any correlations between my own account and that of RBS Shipping Centre and RBS Sempra Commodities, whether any parties benefitted from knowing that this trade with Lakatamia was about to happen. I would also like to investigate the statements of all other accounts clearing FFAs with RBS. If the mistakes made on my account were human/computer errors, or were simply because RBS didn't have the appropriate infrastructure in place to accurately calculate margin calls, then there should be inconsistencies in every account. If there aren't mistakes across the board, if there are only mistakes in TMT statements, then it will be proven that RBS manipulated TMT's accounts for their own gain and that their denial that they notated 80% of the Lakatamia trade to RBS Sempra Commodities was a malignant fraud.

RBS had no reason to block me from carrying out the other half of my legally binding trade with Lakatamia.

Their ex-employee told me, 'It imposed no concrete exposure on the bank.'

In fact, the only thing it did impose was destruction on TMT and potential economic losses on Lakatamia when the market went down and they found themselves holding FFAs they couldn't sell and whose price had fallen dramatically. The story told in the English court in 2011 didn't add up. The facts were the opposite of the evidence and disclosures submitted by Polys. He didn't trade the 7.2 million metric tons with RBS; there was a novation, replacing Lakatamia as party to the agreement with a new party—RBS Sempra Commodities, a totally separate entity, who covered up the RBS LCH (clearing house) short of TMT 7.2 million metric tons.

As I said, those FFAs were worth 600,000 metric tons per month, a total 7.2 million metric ton contract over the year, and leaving them without a buyer was bad for the market. A trade of that size could shift the market and there's no doubt in my mind that RBS' refusal to allow me to buy them back would have spooked the market into a fresh burst of business-damaging volatility. For the first time I realized that RBS were making idiotic, rash decisions that were not only harmful to TMT, but also harmful to everyone involved. The next thing I had to figure out was whether they were making these preposterous choices because of ignorance, or by design.

During this deal, and for a long time afterwards, I'd been nothing but apologetic to Polys. I was embarrassed. My disputes with RBS had forced me to renege on a deal that subsequently lost a fellow shipping magnate money. I felt as though my honesty and integrity would now be in question wherever I went. I felt shame and anxiety that my old associates would no longer trade with me. Trust is everything. Since I couldn't buy back Lakatamia's positions, how would anyone else trust me to do the same? Also, Polys told me he was a newcomer to FFA trading and he didn't know how it worked. He'd never done it before and, on his first trade, I'd let him down.

TMT made $94 million on January 2, 2009, but RBS didn't pay this to TMT. RBS confiscated this money to cover up RBS losses each month. Polys had personally loaned liquidity to what was now a bank owned by the British taxpayer. On February 24, 2009, RBS gave Polys very cheap finance at the Libor rate plus 0.25% interest. In addition, Polys obtained that finance non-Event of Default, to build new VLCC contracts with Hyundai Heavy Industry. The loan was for eight years and the loan documents consisted of 32 pages—only eight pages were disclosed in court. Hyundai Heavy Industry accepted cancellation of the building contracts in 2010. Most people would find it amazing that the RBS board, under government ownership and using taxpayer money, allowed its shipping division to give illegal and free finance to a company that was involved in possible money laundering allegations.

I defended myself in court, not because I felt that Polys was in the wrong, but because of specific legal terminology—to put it simply, he was looking for compensation from Today Makes Tomorrow when, in fact, he had struck the deal with TMT Liberia. A small technicality but an important one since, at the time, TMT as a parent company was being run by other family members and I didn't think they should have to pay for my mistakes. TMT Liberia, on the other hand, was more than willing to face the problem head on but, because we'd been blocked, illegally, from making the trade by RBS, it wasn't a breach of trust on our part, but on the part of RBS who, don't forget, were also connected to Lakatamia.

Then something happened in court that made my lawyers very suspicious. After the second day, one of them approached me and said, 'I think Polys may have been lying when he said he was a newcomer to the world of FFA trading.'

I was skeptical, but he said there were three entities that were part of Polys' shipping business that had, at two points, instigated agreements with RBS. He also said that Lakatamia amended its agreement with RBS on the same day the TD3 600MT CAL09 trade went through, which all suggests that Polys had been making OTC transactions in the FFA market for years. The lawyer also found it disconcerting that, in response to questions about his own personal history with the FFA market, Polys kept repeating,

'We only did small trades in preparation for the big deal.'

What big deal? How could he have possibly known that he would one day make a huge trade with TMT?

The evidence provided on the last few days before the trial didn't disclose details of Polys' trading with RBS for the 7.2 million metric ton position. He didn't trade or he didn't disclose? Basically, Polys didn't have to do anything. He could make $1.8 million if the market went up, and he could make money if the market went down, as he could sell and claim the loss from TMT. A win-win situation for him. Therefore, I believe he didn't trade.

According to court evidence, Polys' 'big deal' was spoken about in February 2008, which was three whole months before I heard of it. Yes, the Clarksons' broker who arranged it may have suggested making a large deal with TMT and Lakatamia to Polys, which could explain it. But that shatters the illusion I'd been carrying with me for years that Polys was somehow the innocent in this situation—the unknowing victim—the wounded friend. In actual fact, Polys didn't close the trade when he should have and that's why he made such losses. That's a fact I felt guilty about when I believed he had no experience in trading. But after I learned he'd been trading for a while, I came to wonder whether he hadn't just been waiting and hoping that the markets would rally in his favor.

It got worse from there. An email between Lakatamia and Clarksons came to light, in which Lakatamia congratulated Clarksons on their short positions—very significant because Clarksons weren't allowed to hold short positions. It may sound innocuous, but it's deeply troubling for two reasons. Firstly, as you might remember, to short something is to bet on its failure and, secondly, Clarksons, as a broker, isn't allowed to have its own discretionary trading account, because it has too much access to the private activity of its clients, so having one would be an open invitation to front-run. If Clarksons did have its own trading account and if it was front-running, along with RBS prop (proprietary) traders (trading for the bank's own direct gain), against its clients, did Lakatamia know about it? Was it possible that this entire trade was orchestrated to give Lakatamia, Clarksons, and RBS the opportunity to front-run on a huge deal? Unfortunately, many of the conversations that Polys entered into with Clarksons were on a private email, so I haven't been able to get hold of them.

I mentioned the possible front-running and illegal discretion trading by Vesalius to Polys Haji-Ioannou—there were discrepancies in the worldwide freezing order filing.

Clarksons claimed a $98 million total loss, but the Lakatamia affidavit claimed $79 million. Clarksons created faked statements to present to the English court in 2011. This all sounds very complicated, and it is, but it's a conspiracy investigation that's ongoing and, once again, will be a subject for more careful scrutiny in my next book. We're finding lots of evidence on the Lakatamia story, as the real data was only submitted to the English courts a few months before the trial that took place in October 2014, three years after they filed for the worldwide freezing order in 2011. The story has criminal aspects of collusion between Clarksons, Royal Bank of Scotland, RBS Sempra Commodities (today JPMorgan Chase), Troodos Maritime International SA (Polys), and Star Bulk Carriers Corp. (Petros Pappas).

The question is, why would Polys want to enter into a complex derivative trade with the help of Clarksons with so much secrecy if the sole intention was, as I believed, to do me a favor? Now I think about it more clearly, without the anxiety of epic margin calls and volatile market conditions clouding my head, I realize that it would have been so much simpler if Polys had just loaned me the money based on the security of one of my tankers. But they pushed the trade on me and, at the time, I didn't question my lifeline—I was grateful. I now believe they all wanted this trade because they knew they could benefit from it in different ways.

RBS had a responsibility to advise Lakatamia to close the position (sell it on) when it became apparent that I was being prohibited from buying it back myself. This would have prevented the great losses and the general enmity. The only reason I can think of for why these positions weren't sold on in a timely fashion is because they wanted me in court. As I mentioned before, if you're in the midst of criminal proceedings, then you're forbidden from entering into new contracts in some countries and this was very damaging for my business.

I've also been informed by Ms Amanda Galloway, who was a relationship manager and lawyer in the shipping department of RBS that, because of their various miscalculations of margins, RBS realized that they could be, very easily, sued should the positions close [disclosure given by RBS lawyer Mr Edward Sparrow re. the account documents]. Once the positions were closed, then it would be possible for TMT to compile the required information and realize they'd been misinformed. For instance, I could have discovered sooner that I was perfectly capable of buying back Lakatamia's positions, that I was actually in credit with RBS, and that they owed me millions in restitutions for false margin calls. (As I said, I'm still investigating this episode and how it ties in with Bernie Madoff and the $3.6 billion. I'll come back to it in more detail in my next book).

This was about the time that another Greek shipping magnate called Petros Pappas attempted to destroy TMT. He was sent information by RBS regarding FFA positions in a June OTC settlement and he made a simple claim which initiated a Rule B Attachment (permits pre-trial seizure of a defendant's property on an ex parte [one side only] basis). Basically, it was an application to freeze TMT's US dollar account and stop the money flow. Let me explain—Pappas, through his company, Oceanbulk, had many FFA trades with TMT. He was also front-running those TMT positions with ICAP. If TMT defaulted we wouldn't be able to trade and this was good news for Pappas. He'd receive money from his positions that he wouldn't have to pay to TMT—even if the market went down, he could still make a profit and not have to pay TMT.

Like I said, it was a simple claim, involving Starbulk shares, owned by F5 Capital, which was owned by TMT. There was a clause that nine million shares had to be delivered by a certain period—the due date was June 20, 2008. However, Pappas extended it to the end of the month to make sure F5 couldn't split the shares. When both parties agreed to buy/sell on June

30, 2008, Pappas gave instructions not to split the shares into 9 million and 3.1 million, as agreed, because he was already preparing the Rule B application to the Southern District of New York, using another lawyer, so the lawyers we were using for the trade wouldn't know about it.

When the Rule B became effective, after the July 4 holiday, Pappas instructed our Lawyers, Seward & Kissel LLP—I have his message to them:

'Gigi, now you can split the shares.'

TMT had been tricked!

I found, in my later investigations, that Petros Pappas was using at least five lawyers at the same time, giving them all different instructions. In his affidavit in the English litigation (*Oceanbulk* vs *TMT*), Pappas stated that the shares weren't delivered on time—he didn't mention his delaying tactics or his concurrent Rule B Attachment application. For a fee of only $50 Pappas intended to destroy TMT.

Being in the middle of all this back then, it was hard to see the wood for the trees—but now it's all coming together. What if Clarksons, who initiated the Lakatamia deal, Petros Pappas, and Polys Haj-Ioannou, clients of RBS and Clarksons, were all willing to attack TMT, in a coordinated action with the aid of Royal Bank of Scotland, in order to cause Today Makes Tomorrow's insolvency and my company's sudden death.

I can understand how this chapter will be difficult for most people to comprehend. Let me just say that all the seemingly separate occurrences were actually co-ordinated by orders that came right from the top of RBS. Every day there was a briefing held at the top level, then orders would be dispatched to the various sectors of the operation. Both Fred Goodwin and Jamie Dimon were the puppet masters, pulling the strings, even if those strings weren't always visible. It was an illusion that Polys, and Pappas, and Clarksons, and all the others were acting independently of what was going on between RBS and TMT. In reality, it was all part of the same plan.

They used me to fix their system and then they tried to break me. Unfortunately for RBS, I'm not one to sit still or keep quiet. Fred Goodwin underestimated me all those years ago when he had the upper hand in his deserted office. While some of my businesses have suffered under their attacks, other projects of mine have flourished. I don't let them get me down—there's too much to do. Shining an illuminating light on the fraud and tricks used to save the world's financial system is important to me but, then again, so is the sea and the ships that sail on it. When TMT shuttered down it wasn't the loss of billions or status that bothered me, it was the ships left stranded in ports; it was the workers and sailors left stranded on those ships with no means of getting home. It was because a beautiful mechanism, like a delicate piece of filigree clockwork, had been stepped on and crushed under a crude fiduciary heel.

This book is not intended for use in any legal action, it is just for perspective. The details will come in my next book. But, when a business as large and global as TMT suffers, it's not just me who hurts; tens of thousands of employees and clients and investors are affected. I realize that's precisely how the NY Fed, the US Treasury, the Bank of England, and the other government agencies that facilitated the bailout must have felt. What a shame the CEOs of RBS, JPMorgan Chase, Goldman Sachs, Barclays, and the other instigators didn't feel the same way!

But what is abundantly obvious is that my company, Today Makers Tomorrow, was used as a key player in the world's largest covert plan to save the big banks from the consequences of their irresponsible and immoral (if not illegal) actions. The cover-up of that scam is gradually coming to light, day by day.

It was too big to hide.

Barclays' Time Square, ex-Lehman Brothers HQ—paid for with Nomura money

Federal Reserve Bank of New York sign

THE DASH FOR CASH

I sat back and looked down at the messy spread of papers before me, rising so high they almost completely obscured the horizontal white board they were resting on. I found the complex and interconnected system of financial institutions, trades, and products easier to understand if I drew them out, gave them some shape, and a skeleton to hang the facts on. I could see then how it functioned as a whole. Even if the collective actions aren't coordinated, they're only made possible because of each other. Sometimes I wonder whether it's important to know if someone intentionally flicked over the first domino, or if it was knocked over by accident. The only certainty is that, after the panic started, a lot of people were making a lot of rushed and rash decisions, trying to save their own skins.

They did what they had to do and then they had to hide the evidence. That much was true in my case and, looking down at the chart, I wondered if it was true for anyone else. That day I was reading a document compiled by some journalists who were investigating the RBS GRG (Global Restructuring Group) scandal that was to erupt in 2016 and is still ongoing and gathering momentum.

Before I detail the scandal that made me appreciate there were many more victims than I'd first realized—that thousands and thousands of people had been defrauded unwittingly, and their cash stolen to pump Royal Bank of Scotland full of the liquidity it needed—I'd like to show how difficult it is to get any criminal activity on the part of the banks noticed.

Possibly the worst anecdote, but definitely one of the most circulated, about the behavior of RBS GRG at that time was endured by a man called Andrew Gibbs—a Norwich-based architect who'd taken out a business loan with RBS and ended up losing all his assets, his business, and his home. RBS GRG was the bank's Global Restructuring Group, a division responsible for aiding failing businesses and helping them to meet and continue their loan repayments. Andrew Gibbs never missed a payment but, after being told by RBS that his loan was disproportionately large compared to his assets, he was forced to join GRG, who charged very high monthly fees for their "services." I've often mentioned that banks have a habit of over-leveraging their assets and making larger loans and investments than they have the equity to support. Well, RBS were now accusing Andrew Gibbs of the same thing. They were worried he didn't have the value in his business to ever pay back the loan. However, this is a claim you don't need much substantiation to support, and it is a pretty wild one considering he hadn't missed a single payment. After just over a week with GRG, the division took complete control of his accounts and canceled direct debit payments, including the insurance that is a legal requirement for architects.

I shuddered when I read about this. I always thought that if I found another victim of RBS it would be a source of relief and vindication for me. I thought I'd feel revitalized in my conviction that I was, after all and despite everything, justified in going after RBS. But I didn't. I just felt horror that they'd destroyed another life. Andrew Gibbs was now, because of RBS' actions, in violation of the law and unable to practice his business which, in any case, he no longer had access to. He owed people money for tools and building materials and the daily itinerary of his work, but he could no longer repay them because it was, in practice if not in deed, RBS' business now.

After receiving a complaint RBS called Norwich Council and told them that Andrew Gibbs was dead. They canceled his business tax payments and took the money for themselves. I don't understand how a registered corporation can get away with behavior that would look callous even for an organized crime syndicate. RBS lied and claimed they had no record of canceling the insurance or tax payments—conveniently, they never seem to have records of their criminal behavior—but, luckily, Norwich Council and the insurance company did. To refuse to even admit what they'd done shows such arrogance and disregard for the law and for their clients that it makes me very angry.

After RBS tried unsuccessfully to declare him dead, they changed tack and played a game of good cop, bad cop. One morning they called and demanded an instant repayment of the full loan, before changing their minds in the afternoon and offering Andrew Gibbs a larger loan, in exchange for 15% of his company. He refused and was evicted from his offices. I'm sure you won't be surprised if I tell you that RBS subsequently purchased that company. What better way to hide the brutality of their actions than to buy up their victim and destroy the evidence.

This happened in 2008, but it wasn't until 2014 that the FCA began investigating it. In 2015 *The Times* published an article about the alleged criminal activities of RBS GRG, as did *Reuters* later that year. But nothing changed. The FCA didn't publish its report and nothing was done. It was only when *BuzzFeed News* and the *BBC* acquired and broadcast internal documents from a whistle-blower—such as emails, memos and minutes—that the government began putting pressure on the FCA to publish its report. Five hundred businesses that had been damaged by RBS GRG then felt they had the support to sue the company. They called themselves the RBS GRG Business Action Group and on their website they write:

> *Individually, we have all suffered at the hands of the Bank and are familiar with their strong-arm tactics. By joining together and pooling resources, we can challenge the actions of RBS-GRG on a group basis.*

The Action Group is an organization their members can be truly proud of. What saddens me is, it takes a whistle-blower—an incredibly brave and moral person—and a leak of this size for anyone to take them seriously. Even though we know the banks are often exploitative, the legal system is biased in their favor and any individual who attempts to make a claim against an organization of that size is going to find themselves in a battle that's rigged against them. Having lost everything at the hands of RBS, I think it's amazing and a testament to human resolve that people are still willing to fight back.

In the wake of the exposé a representative of RBS said, 'In the aftermath of the financial crisis, we did not always meet our own high standards.'

High standards—don't make me laugh! I find this half-hearted apology insulting to their victims, but I also find the idea that RBS thinks they have high standards is comically absurd. What they mean by high standards is adhering to the law only when they have to, and apologizing only when they get caught breaking it.

The *BuzzFeed* and *Newsnight* exposés revealed that a host of secret documents had been leaked showing how Royal Bank of Scotland had killed or crippled thousands of businesses in a deliberate plan to add billions to its balance sheet. Far from helping struggling firms RBS GRG destroyed healthy enterprises for personal profit. The leaked files revealed that, under pressure from the British government, RBS deliberately ran down businesses and, ignoring claims of conflict of interest, collaborated with the bank's own property division (West Register) to buy up, at a discount, the assets it forced its customers to sell. The leaked files revealed that 16,000 firms were sucked into GRG after the financial crash of 2008, including care facilities, hotels, farms, and children's centers. People lost their homes, marriages, and health as a result of RBS GRG's theft of their assets.

RBS managers encouraged their employees to hunt for ways to boost their bonuses by forcing customers into loan restructures and heavy fees as part of a profit drive they laughed about and nicknamed the Dash for Cash. People like Andrew Gibbs, who'd never missed a loan payment, were forced into GRG through RBS' secret policies that had nothing to do with financial distress and which included trying to leave the bank, disagreeing with managers, and threatening to sue over mistreatment. Once in GRG they were hit with crippling fees, heavy fines, and interest rate hikes that could run into millions—netting profits of over a billion pounds for the restructuring unit in a single year. It seems to me that RBS started embezzling money from those businesses as soon as they entered the GRG. After all, they didn't call the process the Dash for Cash for no reason. I know RBS did it to me, so it's quite obvious that mine wasn't the only account they plundered!

After that realization I began to investigate who else had been destroyed during, or in the wake of, the financial crisis. As the GRG fraud opens up, there are many cases to choose from, but I went for the obvious ones. I researched those that had gone down in flames. I looked for the people who had lost everything in a matter of days, because I figured that was a sure sign of a panicked cover-up. I also looked for unpalatable victims, those who maybe weren't complete innocents—who were implicated in the system—because they were the ones with the most money to steal. While I'm certain there are hundreds of thousands of smaller victims of fraud, they would be harder to find because there would be less smoke.

The first one I looked into was, of course, Bernie Madoff, portrayed by Robert De Niro in the movie *The Wizard of Lies*. Madoff is an 80-year-old financier currently serving 150 years in prison for running the largest Ponzi scheme (fraudulent investment operation) the world has ever seen. Though no definite sum can be calculated, a rough estimate indicates he defrauded 4,800 investors out of $64.8 billion. These investors included many pension schemes that left people bereft of their life savings and too old to work—if they were lucky, reliant on the charity of relatives; if not, eking out a pittance from the state and trying to make ends meet; either way, dreading the expensive but inevitable health complications that come with age. His crime had a higher body count than you'd expect from financial fraud. In the wake of huge losses four people have committed suicide, including his own son. Another man, a veteran living in the UK, shot himself in a park when he realized that Madoff had stolen every penny he had. I'm mentioning these innocent men—Madoff's son had no idea about the Ponzi scheme—to remind myself, and the reader, that white-collar crimes do have a visceral impact on life, freedom, and happiness.

We forget it too often. What other reason could there be for the fact that regulators never bothered to look closely into Madoff's accounts, even though they showed every single marker of a Ponzi scheme? He wasn't even trying to hide it! A Ponzi scheme is a simple and easily replicated scam. Here's how, if you're interested, you could set up your own.

First find your investors, three should be enough to begin with, and get them to invest $5 each, with the promise that they'll get 15% interest per month. That's an incredibly high return, but you know you can fund it for quite a while with the $15 you have in your bank account. Pretty soon, word spreads and you get even more investors because of how regular and high the pay-outs are. As your pool of investor funds grows bigger, the amount you have to pay out always remains a small proportion of what you have—as long as you keep reaping in investors, which Madoff had no problem doing. You never have to actually invest a single penny. You never have to worry about market fluctuations, or risks, or reading up on the latest issue of the *Financial Times* or *Wall Street Journal* to figure out what's a good bet and what isn't. As far as your clients are concerned, they're getting their money and they'll continue to get their money because, once you have a big enough pool of investors, you can even return a huge amount of funds to someone if they want to pull out. As a Ponzi scheme, you're more likely to be beating off clients, since you'll only accept funds from people who aren't bothered about looking too deeply, as long as the returns are consistent. Madoff handpicked his investors and turned away those he thought might get too curious. In fact, the only thing that's going to get you into trouble is if you stop attracting new investment, or if too many investors want to retract their funds at the same time.

Or if you get caught.

Usually, you get caught because an investment fund that always pays out high dividends, above the market average, without a single wobble, just doesn't exist. At the end of each and every financial quarter Madoff was publishing numbers that were way higher than every other investment fund. By the end of the 1990s it became almost an open secret in the financial world that he was doing something strange, that the numbers weren't adding up

The people in the know were telling their friends and clients, 'Whatever you do, don't invest with Madoff!'

Bernie Madoff wasn't just convicted of running a Ponzi scheme. His 11 charges included securities fraud, investment advisor fraud, mail fraud, wire fraud, international money laundering to promote fraud and conceal its proceeds, making false statements, perjury, making a false filing with the SEC, and stealing from an employee benefit plan. But, if he wasn't hiding it and people knew about it, how did he get away with it for so long?

The answer has a lot to do with the bank Bernie Madoff used to pool his funds and pay his investors out of. There's no way anyone would have trusted him if he didn't have the implied support of one of the major stalwarts of Wall Street. Bernie Madoff had been banking with JPMorgan for 20 years. That allowed him to cash investors' cheques, to move huge amounts of funds abroad, and to source his account audits from a two-man set-up in an office that was, technically, an auto repair shop. JPMorgan knew Madoff was committing fraud and they had a legal obligation to report him to the authorities. Instead, they did a cost-benefit analysis on whether it would be worth taking action. They figured that it would take a fraud of $3 billion or more for the bank to be adversely affected, so they sat back and did nothing.

During the financial crisis itself, JPMorgan Chase missed another opportunity to turn Madoff in. After their acquisition of Bear Stearns, they realized quickly that it had increased its hedge fund to exposure so, to try to reduce that exposure back to internal limits, JPMorgan Chase did a wide review, looking for places to make cuts. There's no way they wouldn't have noticed such glaring irregularities in Madoff's account during such a comprehensive health check.

As I said, Madoff's auditors (Friehling & Horowitz) was a two-person shop in a strip-mall in Rockland County. As was noted in the extensive document drawn up by Irving H Picard—a man who worked tirelessly to help the people duped by Madoff get as much of their investment as possible returned to them—this was clearly an odd choice for a multibillion dollar investment enterprise, and a strong indication of fraud. If that didn't prompt JPMorgan Chase to ask more questions it's because they didn't want to ask. They wanted to keep Madoff's fund going and keep the revenues and client fees coming in. If they asked and got an answer, then it would make them culpable in the fraud—so, instead, they turned a rather obvious blind eye to it all.

However, just because they didn't report it doesn't mean they didn't have their own way of dealing with it. By the time Madoff was arrested, and his accounts frozen, and his investors left bereft of their life savings, JPMorgan Chase had successfully extracted themselves. They'd taken out all but $35 million of their Madoff investments, and the only reason that amount remained was because the request to withdraw it was not processed in time. Where did the money go? To this date there hasn't been a satisfactory answer to that question. Leading up to this point, they also provided Madoff with unaudited financial statements and made $145 million loans to Madoff when the Ponzi scheme was in danger of running out of liquidity. If it hadn't been for that loan, Madoff would've been caught sooner.

Irving Picard came to the conclusion that JPMorgan Chase had not 'stuck its head in the sand' or been hoodwinked by the cunning Madoff—they were complicit from the beginning and as liable as Madoff himself. The only question Picard had left was whether JPMorgan Chase were working for Madoff, or whether Madoff was working for JPMorgan Chase. In his opinion, they couldn't plead ignorance. No one who's had any dealings with the upper echelons of investment options would believe for one minute that the large sums of money Madoff was accepting and sending to foreign countries would not have been noticed. As Pam Martens of the financial news site Wall Street On Parade published in her January 13, 2014, article on Madoff and JPMorgan Chase:

> *What was happening in Madoff's account was so over the top that it is virtually impossible to reconcile it with a legitimate compliance department unless someone higher up simply shut down the normal bank controls.*

I think that's likely. I believe something similar happened with my account, which is why no one noticed the ever-fluctuating margin calls.

There's a certain sense of déjà vu about Madoff not being aware of how the options and derivatives were marketed, running so many clients who were asking for withdrawals. There's a high possibility his accountant wasn't paying close enough attention to his bank statements. I've read so many articles about the $64.8 billion that went missing, but nobody can say where that money went—nobody has any evidence of how it was cashed out and left the bank. How did that happen? For now, I'm still investigating. But after the October 16 withdrawal of Madoff's entire investment by JPMorgan Chase, it's highly likely the money went into the CHMANEK USDTCM account. This coincides with the beginning of the Royworld Express payment system being used in November.

I'll just hint for now at the recycling feature of the Apple IOS system called Trash—but more in the next book!

If JPMorgan had been turning a blind eye to and aiding Madoff for 20 years, then how on earth did the SEC, the regulatory body whose government-appointed role is to monitor and prosecute fraud, fail to notice? Madoff himself told journalists after his trial that he was surprised he wasn't caught sooner. The official line is that they were overworked and overwhelmed by a sudden boom in the number of hedge funds, which left them underfunded and short-staffed. But it's difficult for them to eschew all blame when Madoff's investors, facing the rumors that there was something underhand going on, assumed the SEC had examined Madoff and given him their implicit approval. They thought, and quite rightly too, that if Madoff was so brazenly breaking the law, the SEC would have him locked up in prison.

The SEC has a moral and legal obligation to make sure that men like Bernie Madoff don't strut around Wall Street for over 20 years, defrauding clients of tens of billions of dollars. In a twist that comes straight out of a gritty urban thriller, it was Harry Markopolos, an independent forensic accountant and financial fraud investigator, who decided to take on Bernie Madoff. He spent nine years investigating Madoff and accumulating supporting documents, but was routinely ignored. He gave them everything they'd need to take him down—not once, but three times—in 2000, 2001, and 2005, yet the SEC did nothing! I recommend his book *No One Would Listen* (there's also a documentary entitled Chasing Madoff). It is a tale of the kind of stonewalling faced by civilians who attempt to reveal the criminal activities of large corporations, much like that faced by the small business owners confronting RBS GRG. Markopolos now works at a firm that sues private corporations for defrauding government programs. I wonder if he's looked into the Primary Dealer Credit Facility program yet?

It's bad enough that the SEC had a civilian do their job for them, but worse that they didn't listen. In 2005 they opened an investigation and sent two newcomers, who were easily awed by Madoff's practiced charm and slippery evasions, to look into the investment fund. For two whole months they spent almost every day with Madoff and eventually came up with a report that only noted he was in breach of a couple of minor technicalities. But then, after the final interview, when they understood Madoff was lying under oath, even they wanted to refer his case to the Justice Department. The scales fell from their eyes and they recognized that Madoff had been playing them the whole time.

So, why wasn't Madoff caught in 2005? He'd faced three well-documented allegations from a respected forensic analyst, there were rumors circulating about him on Wall Street, and now the SEC's own men wanted to take it to the Justice Department. Surely, that should have been enough? But the SEC enforcement lawyers closed the case.

You're wondering how the Madoff case is connected to Today Makes Tomorrow? My analysis of the Madoff case is different to most people's. It sounds crazy, but he had no choice not to appeal and minimize the consequences, considering his situation. A not guilty plea or an appeal would have involved finding out what happened with the JPMorgan Chase account for his feeder accounts in Q3 and October 2008. His distressed accounts may, directly or indirectly, have played a big role in fortifying JPMorgan Chase's balance sheet so the bank could survive and even grow stronger.

Madoff was a billionaire, it was a family business with no outsiders. It was a mom and pop shop system, just like TMT was a small family company and not run as a professional corporation. What he was to JPMorgan Chase resembled closely what TMT was to Royal Bank of Scotland. Many billionaires lost money in 2008 and most of them had very similar business structures. The big institutions and public companies survived, but I'm sure lots of cases of fraud will continue to emerge over the coming decades. The big banks are still trying to clean up the mess, but it's proving to be harder than they first thought it would be.

As an addendum to this chapter, the FCA in the UK has published the summary of its Skilled Person Report into RBS' former Global Restructuring Group (GRG). In the summary, the FCA found "widespread" mistreatment of customers and criticized "inappropriate actions" by GRG. GRG was closed down in 2014 and RBS said it had acknowledged the group's failings and apologized for its mistakes. The Treasury Select Committee chair, Nicky Morgan MP, said it had taken the FCA "too long" to publish the summary, but the regulator clearly has a limited role in commercial banking arrangements. The debate will now move to fill the regulatory gap this investigation has exposed—it's been agreed that a new banking code is needed. The FCA did not uphold, however, what it termed "the most serious allegations" made against the bank.

I'm sure the affected businesses will be ecstatic!

People reacting to RBS' underhanded and dubious dealings

THE MADOFF—TMT CONNECTION

TMT was forced to pledge various assets to RBS as collateral security, as an alternative to cash payments in respect of erratic and excessive margin calls. You have to understand that TMT's positions were, by now, totally locked into and controlled by RBS. On October 20, 2008, Andy Georgiou, the RBS man I mentioned earlier, turned up again. He requested a LNG (liquified natural gas) ship called Blusky as a pledge. This vessel was worth $200 million and TMT didn't have that much exposure, so I refused. But Georgiou kept insisting I make a pledge, smiling threateningly all time. In the end I had to pledge two Aframax tankers that were under conversion from single to double hull, worth at least $15 million each. They were called Iron Monger 3 and Iron Monger 5. Ince & Co were the lawyers involved. Here's the sequence of events:

October 28, 2008: A Security Assignment of Insurances was entered into, along with a Guarantee and Indemnity in respect of TMT obligations, and a First Preferred Liberian Ship Mortgage on Iron Monger 3 for a total of $80 million plus owner's performance covenants. There's no way Iron Monger 3 should have been valued at $80 million or more.

October 29, 2008: The pledged Iron Monger 3 appears on the daily statement as an entry of 28 million—12/24/08 TMT TANKER PLEDGE—and lodged with the value of $14 million. An independent firm of accountants later said, 'It is unclear how the number 28 million was derived or how the acceptable security value appears to be 50% of this number.'

October 30, 2008: Another Security Assignment of Insurances was entered into with RBS for Iron Monger 5, also for a total of $80 million.

October 30, 2008: The entry of 28 million on the daily statement relating to Iron Monger 3 was withdrawn and an entry of 72 million for both Iron Monger 3 and Iron Monger 5 was lodged, recorded at a value of $36 million. "It is unclear how the number 72 million was derived," the investigative accountants later recorded.

October 31, 2008: The entry of 72 million TMT TANKER PLEDGE was recorded at $3.6 billion (100 times the previous value) and no other details were provided. "This is a serious deficiency in RBS' bank statement. Indeed, this is the first occurrence of six rather abnormal amounts. The RBS statements are unreliable and misleading."

November 3, 2008: No daily statement was sent to TMT.

November 5, 2008: The entry of $3.6 billion was back down to $36 million in the daily statement.

November 10, 2008: The entry of 72 million TMT TANKER PLEDGE was withdrawn while, on the same day, two separate entries of 30 million—2/24/09 TMT TANKER PLEDGE—were lodged, with a value of $15 million each (a total value of $30 million). "It is unclear how the number 30 million was derived."

November 11, 2008: The two entries of 30 million were withdrawn and a single entry of 60 million was lodged, with the value shown as $36 million. "It is unclear how the number 60 million was derived or how the security value now appears to be 60% of this number."

January 2, 2009: The entry of 60 million TMT TANKER PLEDGE is shown as $3.6 billion.

March 25, 2009: The entry of 60 million TMT TANKER PLEDGE was withdrawn and an entry of 51 million was lodged, with the value of $30.6 million.

May 15, 18, 22, and 25, 2009: all show abnormal and
unexplained amounts on the statements, with the 51
million TMT TANKER PLEDGE shown as $3.06 billion.
You can see how the decimal point seems to have a life of
its own. "Considering that only two tankers were pledged,
it is unclear why the number of units kept changing or
how RBS valued the tankers. This can be considered as
serious deficiencies and unreliability in RBS' statements."

I'm not going to include all the strange irregularities that
the firm of accountants found, but it's clear that RBS were
playing fast and loose with TMT's assets.

Why?

The numbers 3 and 6 that kept occurring are very
important—$36 million, $3.6 billion, $30.6 million, $3.06
billion, and so on. These two figures will become significant
later in this chapter, when we talk about Bernie Madoff and
his Ponzi scheme. The reality is that the ships were pledged
twice, once in London and then again in New York, creating
two sets of pledges. Later, Ince & Co deleted a lot of the Iron
Monger documentation and, in my opinion, were aware of the
conflict of interest in working for both TMT and RBS—in
violation of both UK and US law.

Iron Monger 5 was finally scrapped in 2010 for only $8.7
million and the cash was kept by RBS for four years. RBS
held the pledge until the controversial settlement for the deed
was signed in October 2014. Iron Monger 3 was arrested and
couldn't be moved. RBS held the first mortgage and wouldn't
allow the ship to sail or be sold to third parties to generate
cash to pay the crew's wages. This gave TMT a bad name and
caused the crew to suffer unnecessarily, by RBS not releasing
its first lien until TMT agreed to unfavourable settlement
terms. This was a crime. The ship was eventually sold at
auction in Dubai in 2016.

But the main point here is how these ships' mortgages
are linked to the Madoff scandal and how RBS were at the
center of the financial crisis of 2008—and, consequently,

TMT was, unknowingly, at the hub of that inglorious episode in financial history.

If there's one thing I'm sick and tired of, it's people in the financial sector claiming, over and over again, that they made mistakes because of the "culture," because of a "breakdown in communications," because they didn't do their "due diligence." These are just buzzwords that generalize and don't go into specifics. At some point all of these "mistakes" rack up and you begin to think, if these people are really so bad at their jobs, how did they get into such responsible and important positions in the first place? It's far too easy to blame "human error" or "a culture of carelessness"—these are nice clichés, given out to avoid accountability. I, for one, am no longer taking excuses like that at face value. Sometimes the plea of ignorance is just a cover for a far less innocent motive—they seem to notice what they want to and ignore what they don't.

I wonder whether the SEC assigned two fresh-faced and inexperienced novices to Madoff's case on purpose? I wonder if the enforcement lawyers blithely ignored their request to take it to the Justice Department on purpose? I wonder whether Markopolos' documents were tucked away out of sight somewhere on purpose? I wonder if JPMorgan Chase were in any way involved? The answer to all these questions is, in my opinion, yes!

Hear me out—it happens in other industries. Maybe it was a direct bribe, or maybe it was just a quiet word in the right ear. I'm not ruling anything out. If there was corruption, then I don't think the entire SEC were in on it, just the right people who were in position to put a spanner in the investigative works.

Madoff wasn't caught until three years later, when his sons called the FBI and confessed, which makes me wonder whether, in this instance, we can actually say he was "caught." If Madoff's sons hadn't spilled the beans would his Ponzi scheme still be running today? Would JPMorgan Chase still be providing him with the cover of checkbooks and credit?

Maybe. Then again, maybe the confession came at just the right time—after the Columbus Day gift that saw JPMorgan Chase receive $25 billion.

Madoff's incarceration wasn't the end of the matter. The FBI now had a bigger mystery to solve—where was all the missing money? Madoff himself reckoned the grand total was almost $70 billion, but Irving Picard has only recovered $1.2 billion on behalf of the many people cheated. Even that small percentage of the grand total took six months, with the aid of the Justice Department and the SEC. Most of it was probably secreted away in offshore and overseas accounts.

I believe that, at the end of October 2008, $3.6 billion went missing from Madoff's account. Documents show how he moved investor sums from his account at JPMorgan Chase (703) to his own personal account at The Bank of New York (621). I think JPMorgan Chase might have opened a secret account under Madoff's name and used him as a cover for their less than legal financial activities.

You see the similarity with RBS and TMT?

I was the perfect scapegoat for Royal Bank of Scotland, Madoff was the perfect cover for JPMorgan Chase. Any accounting discrepancies could be blamed on him, the greatest fraudster in US history, and no one would ever think to trace it back to JPMorgan Chase. They could swap any money they liked and the authorities wouldn't find out.

JPMorgan Chase's problem was, by the end of each financial quarter they needed a squeaky clean statement and, in late October 2008, they had less liquidity than they'd have liked. According to the Financial Crisis Inquiry Commission report, JPMorgan Chase had $93.5 trillion derivative exposure on June 30, 2008—more than Citibank, or Bank of America, or Wells Fargo. I believe JPMorgan Chase used Madoff's missing $3.6 billion to clear up their own bad debts, along with the bad debts of Royal Bank of Scotland and Barclays. They utilized the TMT account RBOSGB2RTCM, which was set up by RBS to move money around and get huge amounts of US government funding, once the TARP had been signed into existence by George W Bush at the end of his presidency. The banks bought from each other to reduce their troubled assets and deleted them from their balance sheets. This was heavily done in October and November 2008 and continued into 2009. (Again, this investigation is ongoing and I'll write more details in my next book, hopefully tying the whole conspiracy together).

As I mentioned before, JPMorgan Chase's acquisition of Bear Stearns left them carrying some troubled assets. So, on October 16, 2008, they started to withdraw money from Madoff's accounts. Since Madoff was also trading in future derivatives and JPMorgan Chase were his clearing bank, it's possible they withdrew money from his accounts using the same methods that Royal Bank of Scotland used with me. Maybe margin calls, but possibly also just transferring funds. Since Madoff knew they had access to all his statements, he probably didn't feel that he could question them without being caught himself.

So $3.6 billion went missing from Bernie Madoff's 703 account with JPMorgan Chase. On October 31, 2008, TMT had $3.6 billion in the RBOSGB2RTCM account that was set up, unauthorized, by RBS. It was then moved from the RBOSGB2RTCM to the London CHAMEK USDTCM account of JPMorgan Chase (RBS originally created this feeder account for the convenience of the Greek shipping magnates and to further its manipulation of TMT funds).

On November 4, 2008, the TMT daily statement didn't arrive from RBS Singapore—this was intentional, to hide the movement of the $3.6 billion. The next day the $3.6 billion was used to get US government money to clean up the bad debts of a number of banks. RBS moved the money made from the TARP, on the back of the Madoff $3.6 billion, quickly around the world in a 24/7 banking system. JPMorgan Chase's CHAMEK USDTCM account in New York was "disappeared" by Jamie Dimon around November

15, 2008, as a "clean-up exercise" of all accounts. All the money and books were cleaned up in the international banks by November 29, 2008.

Bernie Madoff was arrested on December 9, 2008—there was only a fraction of the money left in his JPMorgan Chase 703 account. From December 31, 2008, to January 2, 2009, TMT's RBOSGB2RTCM account again contained $3.6 billion, which suggested that money had to be out of RBS' financial report for 2008. I believe RBS, JPMorgan Chase, and Barclays used the Madoff $3.6 billion in a huge cash swap—the money, belonging to his swindled clients, was used by RBS to buy JPMorgan Chase's bad debts. JPMorgan Chase then sent the $3.6 billion back to RBS, who kept it in the TMT account so it wouldn't be spotted by the Deloitte auditor. RBS then used it to buy Barclay's bad debt, so now Barclays had the $3.6 billion. Barclays used it to show Qatar and get that country to invest $10 billion in Barclays shares by sovereign funds. The banks needed a pipeline to move money around using the investment banking side of the global banking system—and TMT. Where did the $3.6 billion end up? I'll pursue that question in my next book.

The Madoff trial ended on June 29, 2009, and Bernie Madoff was sentenced to 150 years in prison. All TMT pledges disappeared two days later and weren't recorded on RBS statements. RBS Taiwan and part of RBS Singapore and RBS Hong Kong were sold to ANZ Bank a couple of days later. Was it all just coincidence? I'll leave my conclusions for the next book.

But one thing that needs to be explained is the sudden merger of RBS and a Sempra Energy subsidiary, to be called RBS Sempra Commodities. The real role of this merger was to create an accounting pipeline between the world's two largest banks—JPMorgan Chase in the USA and Royal Bank of Scotland in the UK. Cynically, shortly after the EU Commission denied the merger of RBS plc and Sempra

Commodities in 2009, Sempra Commodities were bought back by JPMorgan Chase in 2010—an event that needs further investigation.

I don't find it strange that Madoff immediately pleaded guilty to all 12 charges and didn't once attempt to appeal. It was only this immediate confession that exempted him from testifying under oath—and also exempted the bankers at JPMorgan Chase from testifying under oath. I wonder if JPMorgan Chase had a hand in that? Did they offer him a deal whereby they wouldn't reveal the whereabouts of his hidden cash stash, which he probably wanted to keep for his family?

I find it hard to believe that JPMorgan Chase would have allowed Madoff to continue with his Ponzi scheme unless there was something in it for them—something more than just the client fees, like the possibility of using his account to help them weather the lack of liquidity during the crisis. As Helen Davis Chaitman, a highly respected lawyer, Madoff victim, and author of JPMadoff: The Unholy Alliance Between America's Biggest Bank and America's Biggest Crook, writes:

> *Madoff could not have stolen $64.8 billion of other people's money without the complicity of a major financial institution. Madoff was able to get by with a three-person accounting firm working out of a storefront in a shopping center in Rockland County, New York. But make no mistake about it: Madoff needed the imprimatur and facilities of a major bank. And JPMorgan Chase stepped up to the plate. Why would the bank do this? Shall we follow the money? Do you have any idea how much money JPMorgan Chase was able to make off the Madoff account? Did you know that Madoff maintained huge balances in his JPMorgan Chase account, reaching $4 billion or more from 2006 on? And do you think the folks at JPMorgan Chase know how to make money off other people's money? You bet they do.*

Since Madoff's arrest JPMorgan Chase has been fined around $2 billion for their involvement, but I think they expected that. I'm sure they took enough from Madoff to cover their losses. Otherwise, why would they have loaned him the money in 2005–2006 that allowed him to continue? Because they knew they'd need his accounts when the inevitable crash came. I was RBS' cash machine, but Bernie Madoff was JPMorgan Chase's. They picked a victim whose various frauds, not just the Ponzi scheme, would provide ample cover for their own.

When I was trawling through Madoff's court transcripts, I came across a paragraph that struck me as interesting:

In order to prove the crime of securities fraud, the government must establish each of the following three elements beyond a reasonable doubt: First, that in connection with the purchase or sale of a security, the defendant did any one or more of the following: (1) employed a device, scheme, or artifice to defraud; or (2) made an untrue statement of a material fact or omitted to state a material fact which made what was said under the circumstances misleading; or (3) engaged in an act, practise, or course of business that operated or would operate as a fraud or deceit upon a purchaser or seller.

I thought the bar for proving securities fraud was set much higher, considering how rarely the crime is successfully prosecuted. In my case I can already prove, without reasonable doubt, that RBS engaged in all three. I think most of us could prove, via newspaper clippings alone, that the major banks, insurers, and rating agencies had all committed (2) and (3), so I can't imagine it would take much more digging to prove (1).

But the most striking element of the court transcript is unquestionably how the judge attempted to make sure Madoff understood the severity of his guilty plea. This was not a plea made to strike a bargain with the prosecutors. It would not, he was told, aid him in any way or prevent the maximum sentence of 150 years being handed out. He gave up all right to trial and a lot of other rights, including his right of appeal. His reasons were provocatively repentant and maybe even ignited a hint of sympathy until, of course, you realize that's exactly what they were selected to do. Bernie Madoff took the stand and said: "I am actually grateful for this opportunity to publicly speak about my crimes, for which I am so deeply sorry and ashamed. As I engaged in my fraud, I knew what I was doing was wrong, indeed criminal. When I began the Ponzi scheme I believed it would end shortly and I would be able to extricate myself and my clients from the scheme. However, this proved difficult, and ultimately impossible, and as the years went by I realized that my arrest and this day would inevitably come. I am painfully aware that I have deeply hurt many, many people."

He spoke as if he wanted to be congratulated for being able to shoulder so much guilt for so many years and for now coming forward—but I don't believe for a second that he was telling the truth. In 2008, only months before his sons handed him in, Bernie Madoff was desperately trying to reel in new clients. He was luring people in to fund his lifestyle at the expense of their financial and mental well-being up until the day he was caught. Guilt only has value if it forces you to make amends. If he was fully aware that he was doing wrong and made no effort to correct that wrong, then how could he be "so deeply sorry"?

George Nierenberg, one of Madoff's victims, said, "Madoff's operation was massive, he didn't commit these crimes alone, and I don't understand why conspiracy is not part of one of his pleas. Just to produce reams of documents that were received and the elaborate data that went into them must have required an army of people to produce. And we all know is that Madoff wasn't around a lot at his operation. There were other people that were there who handled it when he was gone."

Another victim of Bernie Madoff requested that the judge refuse the guilty plea because a trial would undoubtedly be an opportunity to discover the missing money and "who else may be involved in the crime."

Yet another objected to the plea on the basis that "If we go to trial, we have more of a chance to comprehend the global scope of this horrendous crime."

Unfortunately, after deliberation, the judge decided to trust that the independent government investigation would cover their enquiries. My qualm is this, the difference between a trial and a government report is that a trial is completely open to the public. It's transparent and we're privy to its workings and its evidence. A report is a basic summation of the facts from the viewpoint of a preconceived judgment, and is often opaque as to its method.

Nine victims spoke at Bernie Madoff's sentencing on June 29, 2009. Mr Ambrosino, a retired New York City correction officer, said with pain-laced stoicism that, "I don't know if anyone other than another victim can explain what the less obvious effects are, how every decision directly and indirectly hinged on the fact that we had the security of our savings."

They had bought a motorhome, sold their house and put all the profits into Madoff's account, trusting that the savings would look after them well for the rest of their lives. They made what they believed to be sound financial decisions that, because of Madoff's mire of lies, destroyed them. It's a terrifying thought and it brings us back to the most basic and central precept of banking: Trust! It shows what happens when we bestow our trust upon institutions that are unworthy of it.

But, as Ms Maureen Ebel, a 61-year-old widow who lost her home and was forced to work three jobs, argued, it wasn't just Madoff who'd broken investors' trust.

"I have lost my life savings," she told the court, "because our government has failed me and thousands of other citizens. There are many levels of government complicity in this crime. The SEC, by its total incompetence and criminal negligence, has allowed a psychopath to steal from me and from the world."

Most of the victims who spoke at Madoff's sentencing were hard-working, middle-class people who were facing the trauma of no longer being able to send their children to college, or look after their elderly parents, or retire.

One said; "May God spare you no mercy."

Another requested that Madoff "serve his sentence in a maximum security prison. This is not a man who deserves a federal country club."

We don't always get what we want. In a letter home Bernie boasted to his daughter-in-law that he was "quite the celebrity and am treated like a Mafia don."

A particularly eloquent indictment came from ex-New Jersey mayor Burt Ross who said, "Several hundred years ago the Italian poet Dante in The Divine Comedy recognized fraud as the worst of sins, the ultimate evil, more than any other act contrary to God's greatest gift to mankind—love. In fact he placed the perpetrators of fraud in the lowest depths of hell, even below those who had committed violent acts. May Satan grow a fourth mouth where Bernard L Madoff deserves to spend the rest of eternity."

It is strong language, but when you read that Madoff stole the funds necessary for a mentally disabled 33-year-old to be cared for at home with his family, it's hard to disagree with the sentiment. Or that a 65-year-old woman was, after the fraud was exposed, forced to survive on food stamps, salvaging from dumpsters, and unable to pay for her heart medicine. Or when the widow of a man who'd invested his family's life savings and died two weeks later came to see Madoff for advice she described how "he put his arms around me" and in a kindly manner told her "not to worry, the money is safe with me."

When I divulge my belief that JPMorgan Chase is culpable in Madoff's fraudulent career, I'm not in any way minimizing his crimes. He deserves every single day of his 150-year sentence. His clients have amassed, collectively, far more than 150 years of anxiety and dread as a direct result of his actions. Only a small fraction of the missing cash has been recovered and many of the people who lost money because of Madoff are still living in penury. JPMorgan Chase is one of the wealthiest and most successful banks in the world and, as Irving H Picard argued as trustee for the liquidation of Bernie L Madoff Investment Securities in the complaint he filed against them: "While numerous financial institutions enabled Madoff's fraud, JPMC was at the very center of it, and thoroughly complicit in it." He posited that they were responsible for "at least $5.4 billion in damages for its role in allowing the Ponzi scheme to continue unabated for years." They ended up paying less than half that amount.

JPMorgan Chase made millions, perhaps billions, from doing business with Bernie Madoff, and yet escaped without shouldering any real blame. They behaved badly, perhaps criminally, but in the end it was a lone individual, not JPMC, who took the full hit. The difference between myself and Bernie Madoff is that Madoff undoubtedly deserved everything he got—otherwise the similarities are still there. The automatic response from these powerful banks and tight-knit circle of CEOs and senior executives is to force a single person, one not in their circle, to bear the brunt of their crimes, both in terms of media exposure and legal consequences.

We, the public, have become far too comfortable with that. We find it much easier to believe that one rogue trader could lose billions, rather than accept that it was the approved plan of a bank trying to recoup losses at any price. Even though, when we really think about it, it makes much less sense in an office environment where all statistics are shared and orders are given. For example, if you want to steal from 100 accounts, it's easier if you move the money to one place, then steal it in a single shot. If you steal from all 100 accounts individually there are too many fingerprints. If you move it all into one account and then steal it, you're less likely to be found out.

It's the responsibility of lawyers and journalists not to take the excuses and explanations of banks like JPMorgan Chase and Royal Bank of Scotland at face value. Their reputations are built solely on their size and the power they wield, not because they've earned it. We must learn to hold them just as much accountable as we're accustomed to holding their scapegoats accountable—because, if we don't know what's really going on in the financial sector, then our politicians haven't a hope in hell of fixing it.

The victims of the banks are many and some, most likely, aren't even aware that they were intentionally destroyed—that they were targeted! It's becoming a far too common habit for the banks and it's a habit far too similar to the poisonous scams of Bernie Madoff in its lack of basic human compassion—lack of respect for the law—and, by dealing so opaquely, its lack of respect for the public and the media. Is it really too much to ask, if the banks mess up, that they should face the consequences? Or maybe they'd be more willing to accept blame if it was phrased differently. Is it really too much to ask, if the banks get sick, that they take a cure? If the banks don't admit to the recurring faults that cause volatility and cyclical crashes, then these events won't stop and our global economy will have to weather worsening financial storms every decade.

Bernie Madoff

THE LONDON WHALE

One final comment on Madoff. JPMorgan Chase held all Madoff's client accounts. The bank introduced clients and received the fees, it invested its money in the same funds that gave Madoff a kind of credit status—JPMorgan Chase co-invested in the Madoff flagship funds. On October 16, JPMorgan Chase's derivative office suddenly called Madoff's office and requested a withdrawal of $250 million from the Fairfield Sentry fund and other funds. The time was up! It was time to push for the cash and the order came from one person—Jamie Dimon. Think about it—the bank had known about all the ins and outs and obvious shortcomings of the Madoff accounts since 2006. They were ready to send Madoff's money to their own equity division and CHMANEK USDTCM was the obvious place for it to go, just at the climax of the financial crisis and the American presidential election.

Given their complicity with Bernie Madoff it made me reconsider another criminal case involving JPMorgan Chase. In 2012 a trader at JPMorgan Chase called Bruno Iksil was making aggressive, market-moving trades in the CDS market, when he made $6.2 billion trading losses. His losses were not incurred because his choices were necessarily bad—although they were incredibly risky—but because other traders, hedge funds, and investors started to bet against his trades, including some fellow employees at JPMorgan Chase. The unit he worked for, the synthetic credit portfolio (SCP), was created to lower risk by hedging against the potential losses of other JPMorgan Chase trades, which involved buying up a lot of CDSs.

Yes, in 2012 major banks were, and still are, relying heavily on the same financial products that almost destroyed the global economy in 2008.

Someone give these guys a medal!

Bruno Iksil has said in interviews that he informed senior executives at JPMorgan Chase that huge losses were coming, but they ignored him. Then, when his predictions came true, they blamed him. He might have been an easy target because, according to colleagues, he was an incredibly bright, book-smart man, who was known for his streetwise naivety and rarely socialized with the other, brasher traders.

Iksil said, "The typical traders, they did not like me. They did not like the way I thought.'

I can relate to that because I was also considered to be an outsider by the major banks and other traders in the FFA market. I wasn't from the West and the powerful Greek shipping community always treated me like I was an interloper. Bruno Iksil was a maths whiz kid from a solid, French, middle-class family and was never fully accepted by his jet-setting colleagues. They didn't like his habit of responding to their jokes about the trading floor with an in-depth explanation of his preferred financial products—maybe he just didn't have their bawdy sense of humor. He never networked or made an effort to suck up to his superiors. No one was going to leap to his defense and that made him an easy mark.

Iksil's unit, the SCP, failed because an executive tried to reduce their leveraged assets and risk to bring them within the regulator's guidelines in 2011. But outside traders noticed and began to bet against JPMorgan Chase, who then, trying to reduce those losses, started increasing their positions again. They shifted abruptly from a unit whose purpose was to decrease the risk taken on by the whole bank and became, because of executive incentives, obsessed with reversing their losses.

The US Senate Investigations Subcommittee report said, "The SCP's net notional value, the value of its leveraged assets, jumped to $157 billion at March 31, 2012, from $14 billion a year earlier."

The problem with that tactic is, once traders smell blood, they're not going to stop. They noticed this shift in behavior and used it to their advantage again, taking positions against the SCP that forced up their insurance. The SCP went down because of trading decisions taken by the whole unit and approved by the higher-ups—so why was Iksil the only man to blame?

The first news stories about JPMorgan Chase's losses only named Iksil and made it sound like he was a lone maverick who'd been making bets against JPMorgan Chase's approved policy. Why were the press even given his name? He wasn't leading the unit, he wasn't even a big name on the scene. Ina Drew, the chief investment officer, managed to retire without her name being dragged through the corporate mud. Achilles Macris and Javier Martin-Artajo, his co-workers and superiors, have both been able to get jobs since SCP shut down, while Bruno Iksil has been left out in the cold. His colleagues told him not to speak to the press after the allegations hit the front pages because, if he did, JPMorgan Chase would go after him.

"They will take everything from you, because you're nothing versus the firm."

The official report stated that JPMorgan Chase executives brushed off internal warnings and misled regulators and investors about the scope of losses on trades. They do admit to mis-marking trades to hide their losses in 2012, but Bruno Iksil has come forward to say it actually began in 2010 when he was ordered to reduce their books. He said he'd been battling against the various policies for two years and tried to prevent his colleagues from hiding their losses, but was repeatedly ignored—a fact the Department of Justice corroborated. Another banker, whose name remains anonymous, came forward and revealed that Iksil's colleagues had been leaking information about his trades in return for favors from hedge funds. This is insider trading and is highly illegal. I wonder whether that's when it was decided that Bruno Iksil would be the scapegoat? It would explain why a group of traders started to target him specifically—and it worked. The resultant statistics did make Iksil out to be more incompetent than he really was.

However, unlike a good scapegoat, Iksil didn't just roll over and obey, despite the dire warnings issued by his colleagues. Instead, he's spent five years compiling evidence about his case and cross-referencing with his own experiences, to try to build a picture of what really went on in 2012. He's since accused Jamie Dimon, the CEO of JPMorgan Chase, of having selected him as a "screen" as early as 2010, and as having used SPC as a vehicle to make money. He revealed that the traders on the other side, who were betting against SPC, were in fact working for JPMorgan Chase and that the JPMorgan CIO (heading SPC) lost $6.3 billion, which led to an ultimate profit at JPMorgan Chase of more than $25 billion in 2012.

Bruno Iksil has since said that his mission is now to show how easy it is for a major bank to cover up the wrongdoings orchestrated by senior executives, by blaming and suing a single mid-level employee.

He says, "The London Whale [Bruno's nickname] event shows that there is a definite price for human lives that remains undisclosed, but is clearly considered by the decision makers. At a certain level of projected profits, a large company is allowed to literally destroy the lives of innocent people, especially if they are innocent but embarrassing witnesses of a scam that is being deployed unbeknownst to them."

He's trying to prove that the London Whale was a cover-up for a trading scandal that allowed $50 billion to change hands in the second quarter of 2012 between a mass of investors and some "happy insiders" at JPMC. And, as I mentioned earlier, JPMorgan Chase officially earned $25 billion from it. (Iksil's London Whale case is continuing and further details are emerging daily. More about this in my next book).

I see many parallels with my own case. RBS and JPMorgan Chase both decided that my life, my career, and my mental health were all less important than their desire to take an easy route out of a sticky situation—a situation they'd caused themselves. They didn't care what damage they did to me or my family, just as they don't care about what they've done to Bruno Iksil. All they want is for us to shut up, which is the one thing we won't do!

In this instance we see again how a complex deceit involving many people is pinned on a single scapegoat to protect the reputation of a powerful bank. I will reveal how TMT accounts and balance sheets were connected to the London Whale in my second book.

The London Whale

THE SYMPTOMS RETURN

I'm not the only one who has spent the past years trying to batten down the hatches and store up the bunkers, metaphorically speaking. More and more articles are appearing in the mainstream media proclaiming what we've been whispering in boardrooms for many months now—the next crash is already on the way. All the signs are there for a fast, deep, and widespread crisis that will be particularly exacerbated in the USA. Donald Trump is making America look more unstable by the day; and the UK has narrowly committed itself to leaving the EU but has so far failed to commit to a single trade deal. When I was in New York last I spoke to the general manager of one of the city's landmark hotels as I sat at the breakfast table, scouring the latest edition of the pink-tinted *Financial Times*. I asked him how business was doing, considering all the talk that had begun circulating about an oncoming recession. He told me they'd started preparing two years ago. So far they'd managed to complete some expensive upgrades to the infrastructure and decrease debt, to put them in as strong a position as possible to survive the inevitable credit drought.

I was impressed. I'm a fan of the balanced budget.

I thought, perhaps this recession might be different. Maybe this time more people will be ready. It was a naïve hope and I realized that almost as soon as the thought crossed my mind. Of course people aren't going to be ready. One of the major warning signs of this potential recession is the emergence of another mortgage bubble, in both the housing and automobile markets, which implies that a lot of people are taking out loans they won't be able to afford once the liquidity crunch hits and the banks start calling them in. The

UK government is 50% more in debt than it was in 2010, and the USA is facing a similar debt crisis. China and Japan are the worst cases of unlimited debt increase. No recession is painless but, somehow, it's always difficult to imagine how hard the blow is going to be until the fist hits your jaw.

As I've reiterated many times over the course of this book, because the banks did their best to hide the real extent and causes of the last financial crash, our solutions were either misdirected or not remotely potent enough. The various regulations and new regulatory bodies set up by governments in the wake of 2008 were intended to prevent a repeat occurrence. Many countries increased the capital requirement that banks need in an attempt to curb the sector's reliance on short-term, day-by-day loans. They also made more of an effort to regulate derivatives trading and, according to Timothy Geithner, managed to cut down the shadow banking industry by half—although banks in general grew post–2008, partly because of all the desperate mergers that occurred at the time and partly because of their unprecedented recovery.

In the UK policy makers kowtowed to public opinion and made a direct attack on bankers' bonuses and the reward-for-failure pay structure that had led to many traders taking destructively risky strategies since they weren't penalized for making huge losses. Now bankers can only receive 20% to 30% of their bonuses in cash, have to defer 40% to 60% for three to five years, receive 50% of their bonus in shares, and the bonus has to be in proportion to their pay. Senior management and traders who are exposed to risk must now publish their pay details as well. However, these changes haven't deterred major banks from paying out "twice as much in bonuses as corporation tax since the financial crash in 2008," as the *Huffington Post* reported in 2014. Neither have they quietened public rage at the still extortionate amounts paid out on top of lavish salaries to the same people whose fight for survival almost wrecked the global economy.

European countries also implemented an annual tax on the banks' balance sheets and separated retail banking from investment banking. They encouraged retail banking to retain enough capital to act as a "financial cushion" during the next recession and protect customer deposits even if their investment arm fails. The UK government has promised to protect up to £80,000 worth of savings, and customer cash is now ranked ahead of any other creditor claim if a bank fails, and will be paid out first. Across the board, the old regulators were shut down and new, streamlined organizations set up in their place. The UK also abolished the FSA and replaced it with three separate bodies with distinct and clear roles whereas, during the crash, even top officials were frequently unsure who had jurisdiction, the Bank of England or the FSA. The USA created a new Consumer Financial Protection Bureau to discourage bankers from selling unsafe loans to customers and to rectify other unethical practices of the pre-crisis era.

Possibly the most famous and lauded of these new regulations was the "Volcker Rule," spearheaded by the chairman of Obama's Economic Recovery Advisory Board, Paul Volcker. Paul Volcker is a well-regarded economist who was at the forefront of both the Carter and Regan administrations and central to the cessation of the high inflation rates during the 1970s. He has supporters on both right and left and has always, throughout his career, been opposed to the deregulation of the banks. I met him at his house in the Upper East Side of Manhattan. He is passionate about his balanced budget but regrets the difficulties in enforcing the ideal of the Volcker Rule, which he managed to pass as part of the Dodd-Frank Wall Street Reform and Consumer Protection Act (2010)—albeit after a lot of prevarication on the part of the then US Treasury Secretary, Timothy Geithner. The Volcker Rule prevents companies from trading for their own gain and restricts speculative practices. This would, for instance, make it illegal for RBS to trade under its own interests in the FFA market, or for Goldman Sachs to speculate with gold, and also reduces the temptation to front-run or to make market-moving trades for their own benefit.

However, Wall Street has been complaining about this rule for years. They want to "simplify" the Volcker Rule and repeal and replace Dodd-Frank because right-wing Republicans believe that deregulation will fuel economic growth—which was, after all, the original mistake made by the Regan administration in the USA and the Thatcherite economists in the UK, back in the 1980s.

Perhaps recessions are cyclical because politics is. If the Dodd-Frank Act is repealed before the next recession hits then it will leave the US government with far fewer options than it had in 2008. It would be without the restrictions on systematically important institutions that prevent Lehman-like failures from spilling over into the rest of the economy. In June 2017 the US House of Representatives passed the *Financial Choice Act*, a Republican-led financial reform aimed at pulling the teeth of the Dodd-Frank Act. Donald Trump believed regulations were slowing the US economy and he proposed drastic cuts.

Dodd-Frank had seven principles :-

1. Taxpayer bailouts of financial institutions had to end and no company could be too big to fail.

2. Both Wall Street and Washington had to be accountable.

3. Simplicity had to replace complexity.

4. Economic growth had to be revitalised.

5. Every citizen had to be able to achieve financial independence.

6. Consumers had to be protected.

7. Systemic risk had to be managed by profit and loss.

The Financial Choice Act proposed to restructure the Financial Protection Bureau. It took aim at Title II of

Dodd-Frank, which created an Orderly Liquidation Authority, designed to wind-down failing banks. It also proposed to reign in the stress tests for the big banks because CEOs didn't like them. The Act was an aggressive bid at deregulation by Trump, which is what Regan did all those years ago.

The Choice Act repeals the Volcker Rule which limited proprietary trading and speculation by big banks.

There was talk in the Senate of breaking up the Choice Act into pieces that could be passed via reconciliation. It's ongoing as we go to press—more in my next book.

The coming recession will be difficult to withstand, make no mistake about that, and we know what happened the last time the banks found themselves facing an oncoming storm—they came up with a plot to shield themselves from failure using taxpayer funds. This time too, they have the precedent of 2008 in which they proved once and for all that they were "too big to fail." In light of this, it's very important that the stress-tests are as rigorous and objective as they can be but, more importantly, that the regulators are not fooled by any financial tricks the banks might employ to cover up their shortcomings.

The price of oil is falling rapidly; the Baltic Dry Index, which measures the cost of chartering bulk carriers and oil tankers, is crashing; world trade has stagnated; Italy has had to provide €17 billion in aid to Veneto Banca and Banca Popolare di Vicenza, as they crashed and were unable to pay their creditors; Deutsche Bank is rumored to be next. The failure of the Italian banks has also proven that the taxpayer is, yet again, the default savior of the banks. Even though Veneto Banca and Banca Popolare di Vicenza are being wound down and sold to a rival bank that still, apparently, requires billions of euros in taxpayer funds. Despite the warning signs there are still dissenters who retain the old illusion that Wall Street predicted "four out of the last five recessions."

However, I like economist Paul Samuelson's elegant response, that 'Wall Street predicted nine out of the last five recessions. And its mistakes were beauties!'

The aftermath of the 2008 financial crisis should have brought sweeping changes to our economic rules and regulations, especially within the banking sector. But the regulations we did come up with, while I wouldn't want to see a single one of them to go, were weak and confused. The Dodd-Frank Wall Street Reform and Consumer Protection Act were so beleaguered by anti-Obama Republican sentiment, and by fractions between the neo-liberal Democrats and their harder-left colleagues, that not a single bullet point was met without dissent. The newly formed Tea Party (a far-right group of "businessmen" within the Republican Party) were determined to try and make sure Obama didn't get a second term, and they were virulently against any attempt on the part of the government to regulate "free trade." They were also extremely uncomfortable with the inevitable tax rises that had to be pushed through to pay for the huge bailouts.

Even though the Democrats had a majority in the House, they still needed the votes of at least one or two Republicans. Because of this, Geithner and his team had to include as many sweeteners as possible for the politicians in Washington. For instance, in states where the economy depended on large insurance companies, they managed to make those exempt from the more restrictive capital requirements. Another big concession was getting the automobile industry exempted from the new regulations that would oversee loans offered by the housing market, even though sub-prime loans were one of the main causes of the crash and the subsequent bailout. Now the sub-prime crisis is building steadily again in the automobile industry and these risky loans are being packaged in what looks suspiciously like collateralized debt obligations—our old friend, the CDO.

They crashed hard in 2008 with home loans that people couldn't afford and, since then, they've recovered profits by pushing auto loans on customers with sub-prime credit, who can't afford them. Déjà vu? More than a million car owners in the USA are already late on their payments, which hasn't happened since the last crisis and, just like the last crisis, bankers have been bundling, betting on, and trying to make money off all that delectable debt. These securities have, according to Morgan Stanley, become increasingly toxic. In 2010 only 5.1% of auto-loan backed securities were junk, but now it's up to 32.5% and, as a consequence, defaults have been rising sharply, which is worrying because a quarter of all automobile-related debt is owned by investors in securities. Real wages have been frozen for the last decade, despite growth in the economy (further fallout from the crash of 2008), and the automobile market wasn't rallying, because people weren't buying enough cars—answer, sell cars to people who can't afford them, just like they sold houses to people who couldn't afford them when the housing market wasn't producing enough profit for the lords of lucre!

That's what happens when you skip on an opportunity to make real change. The factors that caused the 2008 recession will cause the next one, only it'll have migrated into less regulated industries. Lobbyists, special interest groups, and aspirant politicians got in the way of creating a good bill because they knew they'd need the corporations and the financial sector on their side to achieve their narrow and sometimes selfish interests. But if the electorate knew what really happened in 2007 and 2008, then I don't think they'd be so unenthusiastic about financial matters that affect their daily lives and they'd put pressure on their public servants, whose wages they pay, to make sure it doesn't happen again. If they knew the extent of the fraud and conspiracy, then I doubt anyone would criticize a government for wanting more regulation and oversight in the banks, and I think they'd be less than tolerant of the lobbyists, special interest groups, and politicians who, for reasons of personal gain and advancement, are prepared to oppose such regulation and jeopardize the global economy.

They might also have pushed for the prosecution of the banksters who participated in fraud and malfeasance.

Instead, only one banker went to jail for all the dodgy trading, front-running, short-selling, accountancy fraud, and non-disclosure of huge liquidity problems that went on during the crisis. This single prosecution was for hiding Credit Suisse's losses, which racked up to hundreds of millions because of mortgaged-backed securities. I find it ridiculous that only one banker was prosecuted for this crime when it occurred in every single bank that had a mortgage-backed securities portfolio. They were all covering up their losses! That's why, when each one failed, the regulatory bodies in question had so little warning. But, yet again, the person who ended up being prosecuted was an outsider, known for keeping himself to himself. He committed the crime, so should pay the penalty—but it's hardly justice to single out one person when journalists were reporting, with evidence, that the same crime was being committed elsewhere and with impunity.

As John Lanchester wrote about the last RBS statement, before they fell, 'By rights, by logic, and by everything that's holy, it should therefore be possible to see, somewhere in the accounts and the balance sheet, some clue to what went wrong—especially given that whatever went wrong must have already gone wrong, to hit the company so hard less than two months later.'

The balance sheet was bereft of toxic assets and the consequences of bad bets, and yet RBS managed to escape without a single one of its employees going to jail!

If the people, all the people, responsible had been prosecuted, it would have served as a much better deterrent than any new regulations set up. Think about it, what's more likely to prevent a crime? Higher prosecutions rates or more laws? It doesn't matter if there are a million financial regulations, if everyone knows you won't get punished if you break them. More prosecutions would also have given us more court transcripts and a lot more insight into what went wrong. The more suits that are filed against bankers, the more court and criminal cases against financial institutions, the more transparent they'll become.

Timothy Geithner is proud of his legacy and I don't deny him that. Given how the financial crisis played out, it could have gone a lot worse if he hadn't given into the bankers' demands. However, the one point I do disagree with him on is his claim that the US government made back every dollar it lent to the banks and more. I say that, technically, the amount flowing out of the Treasury might have been returned, but the real situation for real Americans is very different. The gap between rich and poor has never been wider, and both the middle and working classes are finding it impossible to maintain living standards that are progressively being eroded, day by day. Right-wing populism, propagated by circulation-minded tabloids and self-interested news networks, is on the rise all over the West because people have had to watch the elite accumulating more and more wealth, while they are crippled and hung out to dry by "austerity." The selfishness of the bankers has, I believe, directly caused a distrust of governments the like of which we haven't seen in decades. Unfortunately, much of this anger has been deliberately misdirected towards immigrants and asylum seekers—people fleeing from the wars and the destabilization of regions instigated by the same greedy elite who benefit from such destruction. For some reason we've either forgotten, or didn't realize in the first place, that it was the unregulated behavior of the financial sector that caused the economic hardship of millions.

Goldman Sachs and Barclays made money in 2008, while the rest of the world saw its income depleted. Royal Bank of Scotland somehow managed to shrink its consolidated balance sheet from the world's largest deficit ($4 trillion) to $3.1 trillion (not including retained earnings). JPMorgan Chase had a $2.5 billion balance sheet though, conveniently, they did use a particularly outmoded and almost Jurassic accounting system (US GAAP) which led to them being called 'the fortress balance sheets' by Jamie Dimon himself. These four banks had a surprisingly lucky year in the run-up to the big bailout on Columbus Day. They suddenly had profitable balance sheets and absolutely great financial statements, audited by the top accounting firms, like Deloitte. The rest of us were on the other side of the US $93.5 trillion derivative trades that JPMorgan Chase made as of June 30, 2008. They took a gamble and pulled it off.

The rest of us lost!

In his memoir, *My Life, Our Times*, Gordon Brown, who was UK Prime Minister at the time of the banking crisis, said that rogue bankers should have been jailed. He said the failure to put the fraudsters in prison has given a green light to that sort of behavior. Little has changed since the crash, Mr Brown wrote, the year 2009 was the turning point at which history had failed to turn and not enough has been done to prevent another crash. The banks that were "too big to fail" are now bigger than ever. Billions are still being paid in bonuses because the banks have been able to circumvent the few bonus caps that were put in place. The banks argue the high bonuses are justified because they "take risks", but we've seen that they only take risks with taxpayers' money. They keep the profits but pass on the losses to the rest of us. In his book Gordon Brown asks why bankers in the US and UK weren't prosecuted as they were in other countries?

'If bankers who act fraudulently are not put in prison and their bonuses returned, assets confiscated and banned from future practise, we will only give a green light to similar risk-laden behaviour in new forms.'

I agree. But I can give him the answer to his question—because they belong to the same club as politicians like Mr Brown and the media magnates who control the flow of information.

Nobu Sue with Paul Volcker

WHAT HAPPENS NOW?

I hope this book will give the reader answers to some serious questions. It's a bit like a war, isn't it? People get sacrificed in war and people got sacrificed to save the banks and the financial establishment. And it was a war couched in the terminology of financial-speak, to disguise the level of casualties. It was a well-kept secret, nobody in the world of financial elitism mentioned, before October 2008, that they'd be printing almost US$90 trillion. The US Treasury and the Federal Reserve called it quantitative easing—I call it The Licentious Printing of Money. It was an obscenity that needs to be properly addressed, for the sake of future generations of ordinary human beings who have to live on this planet.

The financial crisis of 2007–2009 didn't just happen—they planned it! OK, there was an economic downturn on the cards, but it was exacerbated by the behavior of the major banks, in the knowledge that, if they threatened to topple, they could prove themselves "too big to fail" and receive a bailout. To make their plan possible, they used outsiders, like me, to either provide them with the (stolen) funding they needed or to take the fall. I've spent the last eight years trying to untangle their web of deceit and, slowly, I'm accruing evidence that will, hopefully, prevent them from trying to do it again.

For me, the greatest victims of the 2008 crisis are the young people who've been saddled with a burden of debt they don't deserve. They're the ones who are repaying the money printed by the central banks to bail out JPMorgan Chase, Royal Bank of Scotland, Barclays, and the like. They're having to repay this money even though, in their countries, their education, healthcare, emergency services, and community projects have all been undermined by austerity. In the USA and the UK, the great strides taken towards a meritocratic and equal opportunities society have been all but undone and it's not looking like it's going to get better any time soon. In the last eight years, the world economy hasn't grown as expected and now it's stalling.

Nowadays, we can see moral hazard everywhere, but nobody cares because quantitative easing is still quietly giving money to troubled institutions throughout the world. The 2% inflation target can't be achieved in Japan while following the old diagnostic method of economic theory. It's really unbelievable. Future generations will have to pay back these handouts in the form of taxes on their earnings and expenditure—and all this money printing is unnecessary, or would have been if we'd learned anything from the crisis of 2008 and taken proper steps to make sure it didn't happen again.

We have barely, and some will argue that we haven't, recovered from the last recession and now we're facing another. When history looks back at us, it'll record this time as not all that different from the L-shaped recession that tore away at Japan for 30 years.

We, supposedly, live in a democracy. However, true democracy means that a person's vote will count for something— that a free and uninfluenced press will ensure that my vote is well-informed about the issues that concern me and affect my life and livelihood. This will not be true when unelected bankers shut themselves away in a room and make secret decisions that determine our future. The media then clouds these issues by being influenced by the political and financial leanings of their proprietors and owners, leanings that are usually in the interests of the elite few, rather than the ubiquitous many. So, none of the people who are making the decisions or informing us about those decisions have been elected by us. They are an elite club and we're not members. The decisions they make benefit themselves and, when those decisions go badly wrong, the controlled media blame something or somebody else and we all go merrily on our way.

Until the next time.

When the same thing happens again.

You may have noticed that there are some threads to this book that I've left dangling and some loose ends that I've not tied up. That's intentional. This is just the first in a series of books I intend to write about the financial crisis and associated events. The first book covers the plan, the intent, and an overview of the financial crisis. In the second book I'll detail how they managed to cover up their crimes and disappear the evidence and the facts because, despite what they might think, Plan B wasn't perfect. They left a trail. I've also made it a priority to find and interview people like me, and those other accounts that I suspect were used to provide liquidity and funding during the crisis.

There are casualties in any war, people get sacrificed for the greater good; in financial war, people get sacrificed for the good of the financial elite. When the war is won, everybody gets on with their lives and forgets about the casualties. Not in this case! The most amazing story is yet to come, about the missing fingerprints in accounting records audited by the big four accounting firms and submitted to the SEC, FSA, and FSC. I know who they are now, but I must first earn their trust. Not many people are willing to go up against the big financial institutions because they can ruin lives and destroy reputations.

But not me!

I'm calling it Plan C.

I want to leave you with a few of questions to mull over. The first question is, how come the world economy hasn't grown, even though the Central Banks have printed close on US$90 trillion and this keeps on increasing? Second, why are most people still poor if interest rates have been kept at zero for the past seven years? All economic theory posits that those two factors should grow the economy naturally. So my third question is, what alternative economic theory can explain why they haven't? My own answer is that the money didn't go into the economy, at least not in any meaningful way, it was just soaked up by the banksters. How and why that happened will be something I'll explore in a later book.

Royal Bank of Scotland almost ruined my life, with JPMorgan Chase, Barclays, and Goldman Sachs being involved, directly and indirectly. These four major banks survived the 2007–2009 wider Western financial crisis, in one way or another. I only managed to bounce back by reminding myself that finding the truth and telling others what really happened was the right thing to do. They destroyed my company, the combined efforts of generations of my family, to save their own skins. It wasn't enough to demand a blood sacrifice from the taxpayer that they're still trying to pay after a decade of austerity, but they had to go after unaware and naïve clients like me as well.

The fraud, theft, and criminal activity in general during the crisis is woefully under-reported by the mainstream media, which is controlled, for the most part, by the same elements that control the financial sector. It's only individuals, whistle-blowers, and "outsiders" like me, who have the will and the courage to tell the truth, despite the consequences. I hope others who've suffered as I've suffered will benefit from what I write and that they'll respond to my call and cooperate. Together we can compile evidence that will prove, once and for all, the crimes the major banks committed. Once those responsible have been prosecuted we might have a chance to correct the pervasive wrongs that have caused the global economy, and every household in it, to suffer for so long.

Today, aside from the efforts that I've made to bring this story to light, I'm continuing in my endeavors to innovate the shipping industry. As an inventor, I've designed freight ships that have wi-fi so the crew can contact their families and stay in touch with the world, even if they're at sea for months at a time. I put a TMT ship to work during the Deepwater Horizon oil spill in 2010, even though BP made it very clear they didn't want me there—she was called A Whale and had a specifically designed skimming tank that can consume and clean two million gallons of oil-infected water every day. I'm also working on a way to bring banking back under the control of the people it should be serving, through new technology that allows you to run your own accounts and investments on a smartphone.

My life has changed a great deal since I signed those disastrous contracts with Royal Bank of Scotland but, in one way, I probably wouldn't change it. My own troubles have alerted me to the inequalities and evils in the world and impassioned me to do what I can to change them. I know I'm at the beginning of a long and arduous road and I hope I'll be able to continue asking the hard questions and seeking accountability from those responsible, no matter how powerful or threatening they are.

Make no mistake, writing a controversial book like this brings its own risks. It requires courage to tell the truth against all the odds, and it takes dedication to find the persistence to keep investigating. Fear of the collapse of the global economy and the onset of a worse depression than the 1930s compelled the financial institutions to print money. They all closed their eyes to their responsibilities and the consequences of their actions. In the battle to save the economy ordinary people were sacrificed, along with small- and medium-sized businesses. Almost US$90 trillion were printed post November 2008— that's a lot of money! The population of the world is 7.5 billion, that's almost $10,000 for every man, woman, and child. Who'll pay this check in the future?

It's a burden that's too heavy for future generations to carry. Student debts, wage freezes, austerity, dwindling public services, profit-making from privatized essentials, the widening of the gap between rich and poor, are all contributing to political polarization and populism. That's the legacy of the banksters' greed. The true story of what happened is gradually leaking out and I hope this book can contribute to that exposé.

I've now come to believe that all Western bank CDOs and CDSs were heavily traded as new financial products in Taiwan, Singapore, and Hong Kong during 2009/2010. Most investors weren't clued up enough about them and lost billions when they traded. Taiwan's FSC and Ministry of Finance system was strictly controlled by the government and derivatives weren't allowed before 2008, so how were these new CDOs/CDSs now being traded as hot products after the financial crisis? The banks involved were JPMorgan Chase, ANZ Bank, HSBC, Macquarie Group, and many local Taiwanese banks and people lost money. The 2007–2009 Western troubled assets were traded to Asia, then sold to Australia and New Zealand, and then they disappeared.

In 2010 Ben Bernanke was asked about it in a US financial committee. His reply?

'I don't know.'

As I've said, I will be continuing my investigations and my second and third books are on the way.

Look out for them!

Nobu Sue at the British Parliament, Westminster, with victims of RBS and HBOS

THE SEQUENCE OF EVENTS

What happened to Today Makes Tomorrow is complicated, so I thought this recap would be useful. I hope it simplifies and summarizes the sequence of events—you'll find the acronyms explained in the Glossary at the beginning of this book.

1. Deloitte has been TMT Group and RBS auditor since 2003.

2. **In March 2007,** two RBS employees were sent to Hong Kong and Singapore to target TMT Group.

3. **On April 24, 2007,** Royal Bank of Scotland decided to enter negotiations with Santander Bank and Fortis to purchase ABN AMRO.

4. **On May 7, 2007,** Neena Birdee from RBS arrived at TMT Taipei with documents to open TMT's account with the bank. One of these documents was already signed "Prime Brokerage." She disappeared quickly afterwards.

5. **On July 4, 2007,** TMT's account number RBOSGB2L with Royal Bank of Scotland was officially opened.

6. **On July 12, 2007,** $5 million was taken out of the account without authorization and deposited into a New York account at JPMorgan Chase—later replaced and put down to "human error." RBS were testing the water and potentially opening an account with JPMorgan Chase's equity division—connected to the Fairfield Sentry Fund—connected to the Bernie Madoff investment account.

7. **On September 9, 2007,** RBS Singapore requested that TMT remit money to account number

RBOSGB2RTCM, not the swift code RBOSGB2L account in the contract. At the same time, Fred Goodwin, CEO of RBS, bought his third cell phone, paid for by himself.

8. **At end of October 2007,** RBS demanded a total of US$105 million cash payment, without any trading. This was only returned on November 10, 2007.

9. **On February 3, 2008,** Neena Birdee's boss arrived with another RBS employee called Marie Chang—the boss hid his identity as head of derivatives in Singapore. They spent two days investigating TMT's computer security.

10. **At the end of February 2008,** BHP Billiton requested Mattia Besozzi to convey the message that they were willing to trade as many positions as TMT wanted. This was the beginning of the market manipulation by BHP Billiton.

11. **On March 14, 2008,** $54 million was removed from TMT's account and paid back on March 16— RBS were seeing how much they could get away with to set up the home account using TMT money. Basically, by sending USD54million to the FED, they could receive 25 times that amount and return the original amount. The balance was used as liquidity. All the money was in RBOSGB2TCM..

12. **On March 14, 2008,** Clarksons called TMT and said the LCH option was a good product, it wouldn't lose money. TMT entered into its first LCH options and started to trade them almost on a daily basis.

13. **On March 16, 2008,** JPMorgan Chase entered into negotiations to purchase Bear Stearns.

14. **On March 19, 2008,** $20 million disappeared from the TMT RBS account. The money went to JPMorgan Chase in New York so they could get funding from the

Federal Reserve Primary Dealer Credit Facility. The $20 million was then returned to the TMT account on March 30 2008. This meant that RBS had defaulted TMT derivative over two weeks..

15. **Over a six-month period from March 27, 2008,** a total of $484 million was remitted from TMT's Singapore account directly to the RBSGB2RTCM account, even though that account was never contracted by TMT—it was a central banking account used by RBS to swap the $484 million of TMT money to JPMorgan Chase in New York. JPMorgan Chase then multiplied the $484 million by 25, using the Primary Dealer Credit Facility set up by the Federal Reserve, and turned it into $12.1 billion. RBS then returned the $484 million, plus some profit from FFA trading, to TMT's account.

16. **At the end of March 2008,** BHPB suddenly refused to trade with TMT, which led to TMT exposure with BHP for large positions.

17. **On April 1, 2008,** the New York Federal Reserve gave $12.1 billion in PDCF funding to JPMorgan Chase, who gave $11.1 billion to RBS, keeping $1 billion back. JPMorgan Chase got the Federal Reserve money using Section 13(3) of the Federal Reserve Act. As set out in point 6 above, the money was secured from the Federal Reserve using TMT's money—which RBS were controlling—as collateral. Simultaneously, the Federal Reserve pledged $30 billion to JPMorgan Chase if the Bear Stearns deal was concluded.

18. **On April 2, 2008,** Marie Chang wrote a warning email to London, that TMT may discover the set up by RBS.

19. **On April 6, 2008,** I met with George Soros at his house in London. After a one-and-a-half-hour meeting, he stood up suddenly and asked me if he could invest in TMT. I said no, due to the uncertainty in the FFA

market.

20. **On April 15, 2008,** Gerard Joynson showed up for the first time to meet with me and demanded an unreasonable margin call without the supporting evidence—this was related to the LCH option.

21. **On April 24, 2008,** an RBS board meeting in London announced the start of a rights issue to raise £12 billion.

22. **On May 5, 2008,** I had my first meeting with the strange man in the deserted office in London.

23. **On May 30, 2008,** JPMorgan Chase bought Bear Stearns with the $1 billion it kept back of the Federal Reserve money. So, effectively JPMorgan Chase bough Bear Stearns indirectly using TMT's money.

24. **In May 2008,** Vantage Drilling received working capital from JPMorgan Chase with a TMT balance sheet. Besides New York, JPMorgan's Houston office was Jamie Dimon's executive office location.

25. **On June 2, 2008,** I had my second meeting in London, this time with the man in the blue suit. It was after that meeting that RBS and JPMorgan Chase decided to implement their Plan B—which is what this book is about. That afternoon, Fred Goodwin received approval for his rights issue.

26. **On June 2, 2008,** TMT and Petros Pappas entered an agreement for an FFA settlement. Also, a Texas law firm was appointed by INCE, without the knowledge of TMT, by a newly appointed INCE lawyer. TMT's previous lawyer at INCE was moved to the Singapore office.

27. **On June 7–9, 2008,** TMT visited BHPB at The Hague to settle its FFA exposure. BHPB was shocked at Don Argus' involvement in the manipulation of the iron ore market. Petros Pappas also stayed in The Hague with his

partner and planned to destroy TMT in winning FFA.
His plan was to win if the market went either way.

28. **On June 19–20, 2008,** Petros Pappas and TMT entered
a settlement agreement to settle only half of its existing
position. The following day, Pappas demanded to
purchase 9 million Starbulk shares, to be delivered by
end of June 2008.

29. **In June 2008,** RBS carried out furious margin calls and
created market volatility by prop trading FFAs, to push
the capesize ship spot rate to $250,000 per day and then
collapse it to $2,500 in four weeks. BHP Billiton and Rio
Tinto increased the price of iron ore by more than 90%
on its 2007 price.

30. **On June 24, 2008,** TMT met Neil Wages in The Hague,
who had set up the new settlement agreement for BHPB,
which later became a serious issue for BHPB as a public
listed company.

31. **On June 28, 2008,** Pappas ordered the Starbulk CEO
not to split the 9 million shares, so that TMT could
not perform the settlement agreement. Pappas already
worked with RBS to file a Rube B Attachment in New
York, receiving all TMT's banking information from
RBS' Andy Georgiou.

32. **On June 30, 2008,** TMT had a $28 million surplus in its
RBS account.

33. **On July 2, 2008,** RBS increased its margin call on
TMT without explanation. This was the beginning of a
complicated conspiracy to drive TMT out of business
and cover up the manipulation of TMT's money.

34. **Despite the surplus in TMT's RBS account,
on July 2, 2008,** Petros Pappas, a Greek shipping
magnate and competitor of TMT's, applied for a Rule
B Attachment in New York, which would effectively

freeze TMT's assets by not clearing US dollar transfer in the banking system. His reason for this was, we were late delivering shares, which was impossible for TMT to do – so breaching the contract engaged in June. Petros Pappas demanded to cancel the original agreement and force TMT to accept his terms and conditions in the settlement agreement with Oceanbulk.

35. **On July 7, 2008,** TMT entered into a private trade deal with Lakatamia, another shipping competitor and owned by Polys Haji-Ioannou, to meet the huge and irregular margin call being made by RBS.

36. **On July 8, 2008,** Petros Pappas' friend, George Economou, called TMT and demanded immediate payment. Pappas' lawyer in New York confirmed they now split the shares to create 9 million share certificates.

37. **On July 9, 2008,** TMT paid all FFA obligations and avoided default in the OTC market by injecting US$350 million. The plan to destroy TMT by Petros Pappas and Polys Haji-Ioannou failed.

38. **On July 20, 2008,** I had a strange meeting in The Hague with Mike P Henry and other people from BHP Billiton, who reneged on the earlier BHP Billiton request to do business with TMT.

39. What I didn't know was that RBS were working with Polys Haji-Ioannou and Petros Pappas to try to bankrupt TMT by issuing the huge irregular margin calls, invoking the Rule B Attachment, and freezing the accounts, so RBS could take full control of TMT's accounts, which were lucrative. This conspiracy is still being investigated and will be covered more fully in my next book. But for now I can say that RBS were trying to destroy TMT and keep TMT's assets for themselves.

40. **This all happened in the first month of Quarter**

3, which was the most important time for RBS and JPMorgan Chase to survive. The total derivatives of both banks were $93.5 trillion. They may have been "too big to fail," but their huge derivative position was "too big to hide"—more than Citibank, Bank of America, and Lehman brothers put together.

41. **On August 8, 2008,** TMT purchased buyback of the July 8 agreement with Lakatamia by the Clarkson trader Vesalius Kallikaks. However, Gerard Joynson of RBS had refused to clear it, which was a conspiracy between the Greeks.

42. **On August 13, 2008,** TMT had only purchased a 200,000mt FFA position, allowed by RBS.

43. **On August 14, 2008,** RBS raided the offices of TMT UK and demanded an $85 million pledge, without any good reason or evidence. TMT had no choice but to pledge 12.1 million Vantage Drilling shares to RBS. RBS internal records showed they deliberately only valued about US$4.5 million in order to deficit TMT's account. This was found in 2009 bank statements.

44. **On August 22, 2008,** TMT signed the first pledge agreement, but the Ince & Co lawyers signed two different sets of documents that were supposed to be identical.

45. **On August 27, 2008,** RBS created the Silver Street account in Taiwan and kept the Vantage shares there. Meanwhile RBS created 85 million TMT shares (faked) valued at $8.5 billion (the broker account was called 7TMTC and further details will be in my next book).

46. **On August 30, 2008,** TMT pledged Vantage shares were not in the TMT account, but in the Silverstreet account set up by ex-Bear Sternes derivative head. The Silverstreet CISCODE was in Taiwan, which proved the

THE GOLD MAN

use of TMT to shred future evidence.

47. **On September 15, 2008,** Lehman Brothers were allowed to fail, to facilitate the bailout of the banks, due to the sub-prime mortgage crisis of 2008 (Plan A). It worked. AIG were bailed out, using Section 13(3) again. But RBS and JPMorgan Chase had their Plan B, just in case Plan A didn't work—to use TMT as their private source of collateral to get 25 times that collateral from the PDCF.

48. **On September 30, 2008,** RBS provoked the bankruptcy of TMT so they could destroy the evidence of the 85 million TMT shares, even though TMT was still solid.

49. **On October 3, 2008,** the US Congress approved TARP. RBS asked Gordon Brown for help.

50. **On October 15, 2008,** the CEOs of the top US banks were instructed by Hank Paulson and Timothy Geithner to borrow from TARP.

51. **On October 20, 2008,** new CEO Stephen Hestor and JPMorgan director John Macfarlane joined the board of RBS. On the same day, Andy Georgiou threatened TMT – to give US$200 million worth of LNG ships, without any reason – then negotiated to give two tankers, as pledged.

52. **On October 23, 2008,** RBS told Polys Haji-Ioannou that they needed treasury bills as margin call payment, as the FED would rescue the banks.

53. **On October 28, 2008,** Iron Monger 3 and Iron Monger 5 were pledged to RBS. This is where Bernie Madoff's (Ponzi scheme) story coincides with TMT's story.

54. **On October 28, 2008,** $3.6 billion went missing from Bernie Madoff's 703 account with JPMorgan Chase. (The FTI investigation calculated interest on $120 billion over 20 years @ $3.6 billion).

55. **On October 29, 2008,** JPMorgan Chase filed a report with regulators in the UK, alerting authorities that Madoff's returns were "probably too good to be true." Why didn't JPMorgan Chase alert the US authorities? Very suspicious! After JPMorgan Chase withdraws $300 million "to pay for its redemptions" from Madoff's 703 account, there's still over $3.6 billion left.

56. **On October 30, 2008,** the Iron Monger 3 pledge agreement was signed in both US and UK date formats – October 30, 2008 and 30th October 2008. The New York Liberia Registry had evidence of a new CDO which stated the mortgage amount as unlimited (i.e. US$80 million plus owners performance covenants). The same day, Matthew Parker evidenced that RBS had revised the mortgage of Lakatamia, Slagen and Kition shipping Liberia registry to total US$10 million, but never disclosed the truth of the mortgage documents. The mortgage amount is suspected to have been rephrased to US$80 million plus owners' performance covenants.

57. **On October 31, 2008,** TMT had $3.6 billion in the RBOSGB2RTCM account that was set up, unauthorized, by RBS. This money was obviously the residue of JPMorgan Chase's Madoff account. It was then moved from the RBOSGB2RTCM to the London CHMANEK USDTCM account of JPMorgan Chase. RBS originally created this feeder account for the convenience of the Greek shipping magnates and to further its manipulation of TMT funds. The TMT account became a feeder account in London.

58. **On October 31, 2008,** the big bailout (quantitative easing) was agreed by the US Congress, so Plan B wasn't required after all. But there was still the issue of the missing $3.6 billion from the Madoff account.

59. November 1, 2008, (Saturday), novation from RBS Shipping Centre to RBS Sempra Commodities selling 60% of my deal with Polys Haji-Ioannou's Lakatamia to Kition Shipping Liberia. The next day a further 20% of that deal was sold to Slagen Shipping Liberia. This was done without notifying Today Makes Tomorrow, which should have been done. It's all part of the complicated conspiracy I will tie together in my next book, with hard evidence. When novating derivatives, it is New York law to inform the counter parties. This was breached!

60. November 3, 2008, Barack Obama won the American presidential election. The TARP window was now open, signed by George W Bush. But Bush was no longer president, so no longer responsible. Obama didn't sign the TARP agreement, so he wasn't responsible either. The banks could do what they liked.

61. November 4, 2008, the TMT daily statement did not arrive from RBS Singapore—this was intentional, to hide the movement of the $3.6 billion. Then the $3.6 billion was withdrawn from the TMT account. It is highly possible that, by PDCF, this could generate US$90 billion in the TMT account. Public records show that BOE had guaranteed 10% US FED to receive liquidity, which means US$900 billion. The original inquiry report stated US$880 billion was given to UK and US RBS and US$440 billion was given to Barclays Bank.

62. November 5, 2008, the $3.6 billion was used to get Federal Reserve money to clean up the bad debts of a number of banks. On the same day, Polys Haji-Ioannou created a new faked account in the computer system – as if the 600,000mt FFA position was still alive.

63. November 8, 2008, RBS moved the money made from the TARP, on the back of the Madoff $3.6 billion, quickly around the world in a 24/7 banking system.

64. **November 10, 2008,** RBS began internally covering up its wrongdoings, like moving back Silver Street LLC from Taiwan to the UK.

65. **Around November 15, 2008,** JPMorgan Chase's CHAMEK USDTCM account in New York was "disappeared" by Jamie Dimon as a "clean-up exercise" of all accounts. RBS started to use Royworld Express, an internal payment system, to send US dollars to JPMorgan Chase for TMT transactions. Royworld Express was also used in 2009 by RBS to clean up the evidence. The old evidence was already deleted to send to RBS Taiwan, with TMT signature, to package and ready to send further, to Australia and New Zealand. So the investigator appointed by the government could not find this evidence later on.

66. **November 18, 2008,** the Norwegian subsidiary of Polys Haji-Ioannou used Royworld Express to pay US$105,000 to Clarkson Security as a lump sum commission. This proved that Lakatamia's claim had already disappeared from the books.

67. **By November 29, 2008,** all the money and books were cleaned up in the international banks.

68. **On December 9, 2008,** Bernie Madoff was arrested. There was only $234 million left in the 703 account.

69. **In December 2008,** RBS requested further pledges. TMT gave two FFA positions, worth over US$50 million in OTC and 3 million Starbulk shares to RBS. RBS sold the Starbulk shares without TMT agreement. So the next few years of the dividend was not paid to TMT. This evidence showed a Petros Pappas–RBS relationship, as Pappas issued faked shares to cover up for RBS. The 2008 Deloitte audit financial statement was just less than US$900 billion, from US$4 trillion to US$3.1 trillion. The bank had shrunk its balance sheet for EUD900

billion without making any money in its operation. How did this happen?

70. **From December 31, 2008 to January 2, 2009,** TMT's RBOSGB2RTCM account had $3.6 billion again, which suggested the $3.6 billion had to be out of RBS' financial report for 2008.

71. In 2008 RBS, JPMorgan Chase, Barclays, and Citibank were all fined by the US Department of Justice for FOREX price fixing. FOREX is the foreign exchange market where currencies are traded. Currencies need to be exchanged to conduct foreign trade and business. FOREX is the largest and most liquid market in the world, with an average trading value of $2,000 billion per day. Currency trading is conducted OTC, which means trades are relatively unregulated. The $3.6 billion/TARP scam was a huge cash swap—the same rate needed to be kept so nobody had exchange losses on their books. Those banks had to fix it so nobody lost out in the game of money musical chairs.

72. Bernie Madoff's (or his swindled clients') $3.6 billion ($10 million by 360 days) was used by RBS to buy JPMorgan Chase's bad debt. JPMorgan Chase then sent the $3.6 billion back to RBS, who kept it in the TMT account so it wouldn't be spotted by the Deloitte auditor. RBS then used it to buy Barclay's bad debt, so now Barclays had the $3.6 billion. Barclays used it to get Qatar to invest $10 billion in Barclay's shares by sovereign funds. The banks needed a pipeline to move money around using the investment banking side of the global banking system—and TMT. Where did the $3.6 billion end up? I'll pursue that question in my next book.

The RBS empire was broken up after nationalization. The first big sales of the bank were right after 2008, there was a January 2009 announcement of the sale of shares invested in the Bank of China and the sale of RBS Taiwan. Eventually, entire RBS Taiwan and parts of consumer banking of Hong Kong and Singapore were all sold to ANZ bank in Australia and New Zealand for only $200 million—further details of this scam will be in my next book.

RBS Sempra Commodities were broken up by the European Commission in 2009 and bought by JPMorgan Chase in 2010.

The swap between New York and London was reckoned to be perfect to increase unlimited daily liquidity by TMT platform, for the survival of the Western banking system (i.e. move it PM in London to AM in New York). The issue was in Asia, where RBS Singapore communicated with TMT Taipei. The time difference was an almost perfect plan, but it had unintended consequences. It didn't work over that weekend, because Marie Chang had entered the system to report the last Friday position to TMT Taipei. It was changed on the orders of Fred Goodwin. Marie Chang had to print out the changed report as it can only return to the Friday position before 9:00am on Monday morning. The wayward $3.6 billion showed up. In the beginning TMT thought it was a mistake. Even RBS reported that it was an error when TMT wrote a letter to the chief executive of RBS, Stephen Hester, who replaced Fred Goodwin in November 2008. He quit three months after that letter.

That was the beginning of how I found out about Plan B and the rest of the money manipulation. My investigations are ongoing and further evidence of the financial skulduggery will be presented in my next book.

ACKNOWLEDGEMENTS

First of all, I would like to offer a heartfelt apology to the crews and families who became involuntarily involved in this conflict between TMT and RBS. It was unforgivable that their salaries were not paid on time and home arrangements not made. This was primarily the fault of RBS and TMT paid everybody in the end, but I feel this apology is necessary and, as it won't be coming from RBS, I will make it for them here.

I would like to thank the many people who have been involved in helping me to write this book. A big thank you to the many lawyers and bankers who allowed me to interview them, in particular:

George Soros
Bob Diamond
Dick Fuld
Neil Belofsky
Andy Fastow
Ian Fraser
Fred Goodwin
Peter Evanson
Cherie Blair
Paul Volker

I would also like to thank my family and friends from all over the world for the deep support they gave me. That support allowed and encouraged me to continue my journey of exploration into the true story of what happened.

Thank you also to the many quiet supporters from different parts of society who helped in my investigations into the world's largest financial institutions, but who don't want their names disclosed—without you, this book could not have been written.

Thank you to my research team who patiently and painstakingly gathered information that was scattered around the world.

Thank you to the passionate lawyer, Ms Deirdre Brown, who put together the chronological events and advice.

Thank you to my long-term friends, Daniel and Irene Olivares, who advised me regarding how fraudulent white-collar crimes work in the global financial industry.

I would like to thank my mother. I am because of you, Mom. Your passion and wisdom made me who I am today. Your understanding of the banking scandal involving TMT, and your support and understanding have sustained me during a difficult time. You have inspired me from afar and I deeply regret not being able to devote more time to you during the past ten years.

Finally, I would like to thank my father. Your hard work, passion, and love made me the man I am today, a man of stubborn persistence and determination. As an only son, it was tough training, but it made me a man like you—but then, of course, I have your DNA.

Thank you all!

To be continued …!!!

With my mother on Chinese New Year 2011

APPENDIX

I have attached some supporting documentation for your interest and as background to the situation.

.

Stephen Hester
Group Chief Executive
Royal Bank of Scotland

Dear Mr Hester,   *19 March 2013*

At the request of Mr Nobu Su, Chief Executive of TMT and a former client of the Royal Bank of Scotland, I recently met his representatives in London. They briefed me on the relationship between RBS, TMT and Mr Su. In particular I learned that in 2008 Mr Su had entrusted assets of up to $5 billion with RBS including inter alia shares and large ships.

I know from the FSA investigation that RBS under its then Executive Board was not a model of good corporate governance. Mr Su became aware that his cash and assets were being moved around by RBS and its various divisions without his knowledge or consent.

For example in the autumn of 2008 a TMT tanker was listed as an RBS pledged security on 30 October valued at $36 million. On Friday 31 October the same vessel was listed by RBS as being worth $3.6 billion. By the following Monday the value of the vessel was again listed by RBS as $36 million. That is extraordinary and requires a full explanation by RBS. Was the manipulation of the value of Mr Nobu's asset done to advantage the Bank?

Mr Nobu Su has tried to elicit information and all relevant documents relating to the management of the very large sums of cash and other assets he entrusted to RBS in 2008. The Bank has been evasive and dismissive of Mr Nobu Su's legitimate right to know whether his interests and his assets were mismanaged or exploited by RBS for the Bank's advantage.

My understanding of good banking practice is that all customers are entitled to know how their accounts and assets have been handled. Under new management RBS should be demonstrating the very highest standards of transparency and accountancy.

The exposure of the Libor scandal revealed the failure to prevent internal bank barriers being over-ridden and ignored. It is essential that Mr Nobu Su should be given absolute proof that similar unacceptable behaviour involving RBS Sempra, RBS Shipping and RBS Greenwich was not general practice during the management of assets in 2008. He is also entitled to know what 'fire wall' procedures were in operation at that time and whether since taking charge you have reviewed, strengthened and improved them.

As a Parliamentarian with more than forty years experience in government and opposition, I have taken a close interest in the banking industry and its problems. I strongly believe in the urgent need to restore public confidence in Britain's banking sector for the good of the economy. The ultimate return of RBS to the private sector also has my support. It is clear however that much more needs to be done to resolve remaining problems before that can happen.

There is a compelling case for Mr Nobu Su to be granted an investigation of his legitimate and as yet unanswered questions. In fairness to him and in the interests of the reputation of RBS, I urge you to ensure that such action takes place.

I shall be taking advice from colleagues at Westminster who sit on the Treasury Select Committee and the Commission on Banking Standards but I will take no further action until I receive your reply.

Yours sincerely,

Jack Cunningham.

The Rt Hon Lord Cunningham of Felling PC DL PhD
House of Lords, London, SW1A 0PW

Punit Renjen
CEO
Deloitte LLP
2 New Street Square
London EC4A 3BZ

Dear Mr Renjen,

The RBS PLC audited financial statement in 2008 and 2009 and 2010.

TMT Co., LTD, Taiwan ("TMT") is a shareholder of RBS and has been so for a long time.

We have concerns that the statement of account for TMT's account number TMT CO-USD1 with RBS had been over stated and under stated on several occasions within RBS GBM accounts (we can send July 7, 2007 account opening confirmation if required).

The following questions need to be answered in order to determine whether money was siphoned through TMT 0987B account or TMT CO-USD1 account during 2008 and 2009 and 2010.

- The statement for TMT CO-USD1 had shown only about USD900 during financial crisis but TMT had transacted close to USD500mill during this period. The amount credited and debited in this account is close to **USD1billion.**

- According to **IFRS** accounting, it is allowed to **mark 2 market** the pledged shares and ships, however we had found that over estimation of 100 times and reduction back to 1/100 times in several occasions.

- On Friday, **January 2, 2009** in Taipei time **(which means the account statement on December 31, 2008 in London or January 1, 2009 in London)** while bank was closing, the account had showed USD3,600,000,000. The bank was closed on January 1 and 2nd all over the world. How could this have happened?

These potentially make the Financial Statements of RBS PLC and RBS Greenwich Capitals wrong.

We have further written to the Chief Executive and former Non Executive of RBS PLC who had handled the clean up and the rescuing RBS from bankruptcy during the financial crisis.

As the all above incidents were after **Bank of England bought 79.9pct of RBS PLC,** we are very concerned whether the largest shareholders of British Government is aware of this strange evidences of financial statement.

According to Financial Conduct Authority new regulations, TMT Co., LTD, Taiwan (as the one of the shareholders in RBS PLC in UK and RBS ADR in NYSE), we demand a proper explanation by November 30, 2015.

Kind regards,

Nobu Su
Chairman
TMT Co., Ltd.

TODAY MAKES TOMORROW

Punit Renjen
CEO
Deloitte LLP
2 New Street Square
London EC4A 3BZ

4th July 2016

Dear Sirs,

We refer to the attached correspondence to which we have received no response. We therefore send copies to members of the board.

The issues raised are serious in our view and although you may wish to bury this episode under the carpet your position in Deloitte and your professional obligations behove you to investigate matter.

Please will Deloitte respond within 14 days.

Kind regards,

Nobu Su

Chairman
TMT Co., Ltd.

CC relevant board members

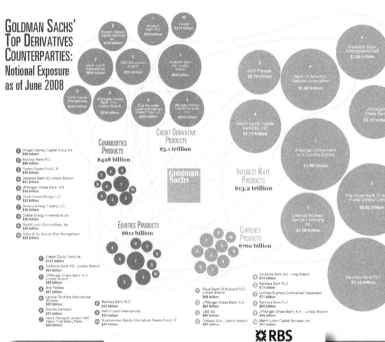

The Smoking Gun (personal details edited)

From: JOYNSON, Gerard, GBM
Sent: 09/30/2008 11:21:43
To: WARWICK, Lorraine, GBM; WATTERS, Martin, GBM
Subject: Re: TMT account summary cob 29th Sep 2008
I agree totally, have told them that they can have neither. Posession being better than anything and if necessary we could provoke a default event which would ensure that we hold everything until we close it out.
----- Original Message -----
From: WARWICK, Lorraine, GBM
To: TRAVIS, James, GBM; GEORGIOU, Andy, GBM
Cc: JOYNSON, Gerard, GBM; KNOTTENBELT, William, GBM; LUXTON, Steve, GBM; NORTH, Debbie, GBM; MUKASA, George, GBM; WATTERS, Martin, GBM
Sent: Tue Sep 30 12:18:49 2008
Subject: RE: TMT account summary cob 29th Sep 2008
Dear All,
As a Credit condition this facility was agreed on a cash secured basis, if legally we are required to release security in the event of over-collateralisation we should retain the cash and release the shares if necessary.
Regards, Lorraine Warwick
RBS Global Banking & Markets

From: TRAVIS, James, GBM
Sent: 30 September 2008 11:14
To: GEORGIOU, Andy, GBM; MUKASA, George, GBM; WATTERS, Martin, GBM
Cc: JOYNSON, Gerard, GBM; KNOTTENBELT, William, GBM; LUXTON, Steve, GBM; NORTH, Debbie, GBM; WARWICK, Lorraine, GBM
Subject: RE: TMT account summary cob 29th Sep 2008
Andy, I can confirm that the initial margin reduced as follows:
C.O.B 26/09/08 = USD 41,741,557.00 DR
C.O.B 29/09/08 = USD 39,871,295.00 DR
Additionally,we are taking in trades that reduce the position/margin and have managed to reduce overall IM exposure from 58,172,392.00 DR as at the 01/09/08. However, should TMT not trade throughout the day or trade a minimal size liquidating trade, the IM may appear to increase due to fluctuations in the NLV on the options that is included in the IM figure.
To clarify the below, from the expiry,we will receive $ 4,262,169.00 in initial margin back tonight and based on last night's prices potentially an additional $3,010,194.00. This would take the account balance to a credit of $6,138,449.25 prior to the inclusion of the collateral and return the account to an overall credit.
Many thanks, James Travis
RBS Global Banking & Markets

From: GEORGIOU, Andy, GBM
Sent: 30 September 2008 10:59
To: TRAVIS, James, GBM; MUKASA, George, GBM; WATTERS, Martin, GBM
Cc: JOYNSON, Gerard, GBM; KNOTTENBELT, William, GBM; LUXTON, Steve, GBM; NORTH, Debbie, GBM; WARWICK, Lorraine, GBM
Subject: RE: TMT account summary cob 29th Sep 2008
James
thanks
Can I ask why the IM is going up not down? Can you also confirm that we are only accepting close out trades not new trades
Apologies if these are obvious questions
Regards
Andy Georgiou
RBS Global Banking & Markets

From: TRAVIS, James, GBM
Sent: 30 September 2008 10:36
To: MUKASA, George, GBM; GEORGIOU, Andy, GBM; WATTERS, Martin, GBM
Cc: JOYNSON, Gerard, GBM; KNOTTENBELT, William, GBM; LUXTON, Steve, GBM; NORTH, Debbie, GBM
Subject: TMT account summary cob 29th Sep 2008
All, TMT have the following balances in their account today:
Ending cash - USD 5,785,689.25 DR
VM - USD 44,523,070.50 CR
Total Equity - 38,737,381.25 CR
IM - USD 39,871,295.00 DR
Deficit equity - USD 1,133,913.75 DR
Additionally to the above, we hold collateral to the value of $ 11,110,715.07 CR with 70 % haircut, based on the EDSP for last night of 3.05 ,resulting in overall current total value is $ 37,035,716.90 CR
Thus total excess equity inclusive of collateral is $ 9,976,801.32 CR
With regards the above, yesterday's trading actually reduced the Initial margin requirement by $1.9 million, however we saw a devaluation in the variation margin to the value of $3.05 million, thus taking TMT into an overall equity debit. Using the collateral to offset the IM would result in the overall credit balance above.
Furthermore, today is the last traded day for all September positions and the expiry will release the following value should it take place at last night's closing price:

Product	IM	VM	Total Margin
Sep-08			
TD3	3,059,000.00	3,083,977.00	6,142,977.0
TD5	245,000.00	919,277.00	1,164,277.00
TD7	154,000.00	506,430.00	660,430.00
CTC	25,000.00	7,770.00	32,770.00
CTCO	749,964.00	-1,673,010.00	-923,046.00
PTCO	-	-	-
HTC	29,205.00	165,750.00	194,955.00
Total	4,262,169.00	3,010,194.00	
7,272,363.00 CR			

I will provide further updates daily and please do not hesitate to contact me should you require any further information.
Many thanks, James Travis
RBS Global Banking & Markets

Financial Times, September 9, 2013

FINANCIAL TIMES MONDAY SEPTEMBER 9 2013

FIXING FINANCE

Watchdogs can claim partial victory on tackling the causes of the financial crisis, writes **Patrick Jenkins**

Banks adapt to being kept in check

LEHMAN'S LEGACY

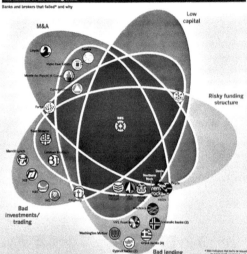

The nucleus of the banking crisis
Banks and brokers that failed* and why

M&A

Low capital

Risky funding structure

Bad investments/ trading

Bad lending

34

The number of big banks that failed in the global financial crisis

$2.4tn

Amount of assets held by JPMorgan, compared with $1.64tn in 2007

ON FT.COM

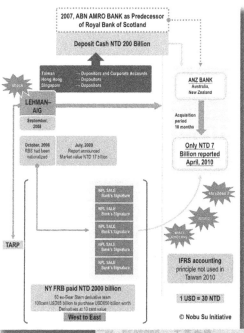

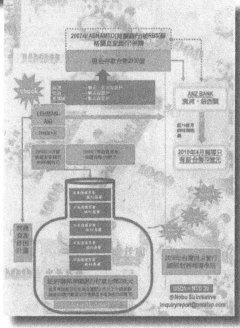

US$3.6 billion in Financial Crisis and important chlonological.

Pre October 2008

September 31, 2008, TMT Was provoked default and 85mill shares disappeared. Then October 1, the 12.1mill Vantage shares entry to TMT account. Silver STreet kept vantage shares.

From:	JOYNSON, Gerard, GBM
Sent:	09/30/2008 11:21:43
To:	WARWICK, Lorraine, GBM; WATTERS, Martin, GBM
Subject:	Re: TMT account summary cob 29th Sep 2008

I agree totally, have told them that they can have neither. Posession being better than anything and if necessary we could provoke a default event which would ensure that we hold everything until we close it out.

----- Original Message -----
From: WARWICK, Lorraine, GBM
To: TRAVIS, James, GBM; OEORGIOU, Andy, GBM
Cc: JOYNSON, Gerard, GBM; KNOTTENBELT, William, GBM; LUXTON, Steve, GBM; NORTH, Debbie, GBM; MUKASA, George, GBM; WATTERS, Martin, GBM
Sent: Tue Sep 30 12:18:49 2008
Subject: RE: TMT account summary cob 29th Sep 2008

Dear All,

As a Credit condition this facility was agreed on a cash secured basis, if legally we are required to release security in the event of over-collateralisation we should retain the cash and release the shares if necessary.

Regards

Lorraine Warwick
RBS Global Banking & Markets
Office: +44 20 7085 3010

Authorised & Regulated by the

Financial Services Authority

```
TMT CO LTD                              Account Number:    09878

8F NO 126 SEC 1 JIANGUO N.RD            Statement Date: 01 OCT 2008

TAIPEI                                  Tax ID:

TAIWAN

FFA CLEARING ACCOUNT

09878
```

Page 37

```
* * * * * * * * * * * O P E N   P O S I T I O N S * * * * * * * * * * *
TRADE DATE   SETL   AT   LONG   SHORT   CONTRACT DESCRIPTION               EX   TRADE PRICE   CC   DEBIT/CREDIT
-----------  ----   --   -----  -----   -------------------------------   ---- -----------   ---  ----------------
26/03/08                           31 DEC/08   PANAMAX TC AVG 4 OP CALL 70000.0 ENCL   5680.0000   USD    6,479.00DR
10/04/08                           31 DEC/08   PANAMAX TC AVG 4 OP CALL 70000.0 ENCL   5250.0000   USD    6,479.00DR
EX-31/12/08               *   62*                                 SETTLEMENT PX    209.0000          12,958.00DR
26/03/08                           31 OCT/08   PANAMAX TC AVG 4 OP CALL 71500.0 ENCL   6150.0000   USD    3.10DR
EX-31/10/08               *   31*                                 SETTLEMENT PX      0.1000           3.10DR
26/03/08                           30 NOV/08   PANAMAX TC AVG 4 OP CALL 71500.0 ENCL   6150.0000   USD    1,530.00DR
EX-30/11/08               *   30*                                 SETTLEMENT PX     51.0000           1,530.00DR
26/03/08                           31 DEC/08   PANAMAX TC AVG 4 OP CALL 71500.0 ENCL   6150.0000   USD    5,859.00DR
EX-31/12/08               *   31*                                 SETTLEMENT PX    185.0000           5,859.00DR


22/06/08           12142858   *   PHYSICAL TMT SHARES PLEDGE                             USD 10,892,143.63CR
```

RBS Greenwich Futures

The Royal Bank of Scotland plc

Trading as RBS Greenwich Futures

135 BISHOPSGATE

LONDON EC2M 3UR

Authorised & Regulated by the

Financial Services Authority

TMT CO LTD   Account Number: 09878

8F NO 126 SEC 1 JIANGUO N.RD   Statement Date: 31 OCT 2008

TAIPEI   Tax ID:

TAIWAN

FFA CLEARING ACCOUNT

09878

Page 1

* * * * * * * * * * * * * * A C C O U N T   S U M M A R Y * * * * * * * * * * * * * *

US DOLLAR

BEGINNING CASH BALANCE	18,385,832.25CR
COMMISSION	0.00
GROSS PROFIT OR LOSS	3,776,536.00CR
OPTION PREMIUM	0.00
CASH AMOUNTS	0.00
ENDING BALANCE	22,162,368.25CR
FORWARD CASH	0.00
FORWARD P&L/PREM/COMMISSION	0.00
FUTURES VARIATION MARGIN	7,094,254.50CR
OPTIONS VARIATION MARGIN	0.00
TOTAL EQUITY	29,256,622.75CR
SECURITIES ON DEPOSIT	3,600,000,000.00CR
NET LIQUIDATING VALUE (FOV)	90,786,986.50DR
INITIAL MARGIN REQUIRED	12,130,159.00DR
CONTINGENT MARGIN	0.00
EXCESS/DEFICIT	17,126,463.75CR
EXCHANGE RATE TO BASE	1

* * * * * * * * * * * * * * S E T T L E M E N T S * * * * * * * * * * * * * * * *

TRADE DATE	SETL	AT	LONG	SHORT	CONTRACT DESCRIPTION	EX	TRADE PRICE	CC	DEBIT/CREDIT
11/10/07				15	OCT 08 LCH OTC BALTIC TD3	ENCL	13.1765	USD	
30/10/07			30		OCT 08 LCH OTC BALTIC TD3	ENCL	14.0790	USD	
31/10/07			20		OCT 08 LCH OTC BALTIC TD3	ENCL	14.0790	USD	
08/11/07			5		OCT 08 LCH OTC BALTIC TD3	ENCL	14.2595	USD	
20/11/07			10		OCT 08 LCH OTC BALTIC TD3	ENCL	15.5230	USD	
22/11/07			5		OCT 08 LCH OTC BALTIC TD3	ENCL	15.7035	USD	
11/12/07			20		OCT 08 LCH OTC BALTIC TD3	ENCL	17.6890	USD	

Please report any differences immediately. The failure to immediately exercise your right to
have errors corrected will be deemed your agreement that this statement is correct and ratified.

To KPMG Group Auditors

This is to certify that I, Polys Haji-Ioannou, have undertaken forward freight agreements
(FFA's) in accordance with the below schedule of trades in 2008 through the relevant UK
market for trading, vis the London Clearing House (LCH) for my sole benefit and at my
entire risk.

Schedule of Trades:
On 11th June 2008: Purchase of 50kt FFA, cal'09 vlcc td3 route at WS 95.47
(Comm.0.4%)
On 8th July 2008: Purchase of 600kt FFA, cal'09, vlcc td3 route at WS 100.65
(net with RBS)
In period July to 31st December 2008:
Sale of 200kt FFA, cal'09 vlcc td3 route at various WS.
In July 2008
Agreement (private) for cover re. 600kt vlcc td3 route at WS101.45

Position on 31st December 2008:
Open Trades 450kt FFA, cal'09 vlcc td3 route at valuation of WS 38
Agreement for cover at fixed rate; WS101.45, giving net of WS 0.4, after commission
Closed Trades 200kt FFA cal'09 vlcc td3 for settlement in 2009.

I certify that the results and position of the above trades, due for settlement in 2009, have
been matched by such deals as per the agreement (private) which provides for a surplus
on trading.

INVOLVEMENT OF CYCLOPS SHIPS LTD AND ITS SUBSIDIARIES
This is to confirm that I have authorized and approved the use of three of the subsidiaries
of my shipping group, Cyclops Ships Ltd, to provide banking facilities, including ISDA
Margin Agreements and Supplements with the Royal Bank of Scotland plc (RBS), in
support of the above-scheduled trades.
The resulting Margin requirements which, in view of the agency arrangement between
myself and the subsidiaries dated 15 May 2003, have not been recorded in the books of
the (3) subsidiaries, amount to a total of United States Dollars 86.640.810,56 being held
by RBS on 31st December 2008, and I hereby certify that the eventual use of these funds
will be entirely funded from the agreement (private) and the supply of capital from
personal sources, in accordance with my existing commitments to Cyclops Ships Ltd and
the Group.

Signed this day 13th May 2009,
By Mr Polys Haji-Iannou

Rule B Attachment (p.1)

Case 13-33763   Document 2300-5   Filed in TXSB on 01/23/15   Page 1 of 3
U.S. District Court
Exhibit E
Southern District of New York (Foley Square)
CIVIL DOCKET FOR CASE #: 1:08-cv-06145-VM

Oceanbulk Shipping & Trading S.A. v. Taiwan Maritime Transport Co. Ltd. et al.
Assigned to: Judge Victor Marrero
Cause: 28:1333ad Admiralty

Date Filed: 07/03/2008
Date Terminated: 02/04/2010
Jury Demand: None
Nature of Suit: 120 Contract: Marine
Jurisdiction: Federal Question

Plaintiff
ABC
TERMINATED: 02/04/2010

Plaintiff
Oceanbulk Shipping & Trading S.A.

represented by **Charles Platto**
Law Office of Charles Platto
1020 Park Avenue
Suite 6B
New York, NY 10028
(212) 423-0579
Fax: (212) 423-0590
Email: cplatto@plattolaw.com
LEAD ATTORNEY
ATTORNEY TO BE NOTICED

Joseph G. Grasso
Wiggin and Dana LLP
2 Stamford Plaza
281 Tresser Blvd.
Stamford, CT 06901
(212) 490-1700
Fax: (212) 490-0536
Email: jgrasso@wiggin.com
LEAD ATTORNEY
ATTORNEY TO BE NOTICED

Scott R. Greathead
Wiggin and Dana LLP(New York)
450 Lexington Avenue, Suite 3800
New York, NY 10017
(212) -551-2615
Fax: (212)-490-0536
Email: sgreathead@wiggin.com
LEAD ATTORNEY
ATTORNEY TO BE NOTICED

V.

Defendant
DEF
TERMINATED: 02/04/2010

Defendant
Taiwan Maritime Transport Co. Ltd.

Defendant
TMT Co., Ltd

Defendant
TMT Asia Ltd.

Rule B Attachment (p.2)

Defendant

3 Capital

Defendant

5 Capital

Date Filed	#	Docket Text
07/03/2008	1	ORDER. Case sealed. (Signed by Judge Sidney H. Stein on 7/3/2008) (rt) Modified on 7/7/2008 (rt). (Entered: 07/07/2008)
07/03/2008		Magistrate Judge James C. Francis IV is so designated. (rt) (Entered: 07/07/2008)
12/04/2010	4	ORDERED, that the Clerk of Court is directed to unseal the case. (Signed by Judge Victor Marrero on 02/04/2010) (jri) (Entered: 02/04/2010)
12/04/2010	5	ORDER that the Clerk of Court is directed to unseal the case and that the case is to remain closed. (Signed by Judge Victor Marrero on 2/4/10) (cd) (Entered: 02/04/2010)
12/04/2010		Minute Entry for proceedings held before Judge Victor Marrero: Telephone Conference held on 2/4/2010. Plaintiff does not object to unsealing of record. (mro) (Entered: 02/08/2010)
12/04/2010	6	ORDER GRANTING PLAINTIFF'S REQUEST TO FILE DOCUMENTS UNDER SEAL: It is hereby ORDERED that the Clerk of this Court is directed to retain Plaintiff's Rule B application and all attendant pleadings in the above-captioned matter under seal until the earlier of this Court directing otherwise or the attachment of property in this action; and it is further ORDERED that the Plaintiff shall notify this Court in writing as soon as it has served the Rule B Order of Attachment on all known garnishees in possession of Defendants' assets sufficient to secure Plaintiff's claims and request that the seal be lifted. (Signed by Judge Sidney H. Stein on 7/3/2008) (This Order was sealed in envelope #2 and unsealed with Order #4.)(jfe) (Entered: 02/22/2010)
12/04/2010	7	COMPLAINT against Taiwan Maritime Transport Co. Ltd., TMT Co., Ltd, TMT Asia Ltd., F3 Capital, F5 Capital. (Filing Fee $ 350.00, Receipt Number 655818)Document filed by Oceanbulk Shipping & Trading S.A..(This Order was sealed in envelope #2 and unsealed with Order #4.)(jfe) (Entered: 02/22/2010)
12/04/2010	8	RULE 7.1 CORPORATE DISCLOSURE STATEMENT. No Corporate Parent. Document filed by Oceanbulk Shipping & Trading S.A..(This Order was sealed in envelope #2 and unsealed with Order #4.)(jfe) (Entered: 02/22/2010)
12/04/2010	9	ORDER OF ATTACHMENT: It is hereby ORDERED that the Clerk of this Court is directed forthwith to issue the Process of Maritime Attachment and Garnishment for seizure of all tangible and intangible property of the Defendants, as described herein, including but not limited to shares of Star Bulk Cariers Corp. issued to F5 Capital, as the nominee of Defendant TMT Co., shares of Vantage Energy Services, Inc. and/or Vantage Drilling Company issued to F3 Capital, as the nominee of Defendant TMT Co., and any other property of the Defendants (collectively, the "Assets"), as may be held, received or transferred in their name or for their benefit at, moving through, or within the possession, custody or control of any entity in this District, including but not limited to Dahlman Rose & Company; American Stock Transfer & Trust Company; Ellenoff Grossman & Schole LLP; ABN-AMRO; American Express Ban; Bank of America; Bank of New York; Deutsche Ban; Citibank; HSBC Ban USA, N.A.; J.P. Morgan Chase; Standard Chartered Bank, Wachovia Bank, N.A. and/or other garnishee(s) on whom a copy of the Process of Maritime Attachment and Garnishment may be served in the amount up to and including $248,879,074.00 pursuant to Rule B of the Supplemental Rules for Admiralty and Maritime Claims of the Federal Rules of Civil Procedure. It is further ORDERED that Joseph G. Grasso, or any other partner, associate, paralegal or other agent of Wiggin and Dana LLP be and is hereby appointed, in addition to the United States Marshal, to serve the Process of Attachment and Garnishment and the Verified Complaint, together with a copy of this Order and any interrogatories, upon any garnishee named in the Process, together with any other garnishee(s) who (based upon information developed subsequent hereto by the Plaintiff) may hold assets of, for, or on behalf of any of Defendants. The Writ of Maritime Attachment and Garnishment authorized herein shall remain in effect for an initial period of ninety (90) days. Prior to its expiration plaintiff may request renewal upon showing of sufficient reason to maintain this Order in place. Plaintiff shall provide the Court with a report on the status of this matter within ninety (90) days from the date of this Order. In the event such report or application for renewal is not as specified, the Court may dismiss the action. So Ordered (Signed by Judge Victor Marrero on 2/3/2008) (This Order was sealed in envelope #2 and unsealed with Order #4.)(jfe) (Entered: 02/22/2010)
12/04/2010	10	DECLARATION of Joseph G. Grasso re: 9 Order of Attachment. Document filed by Oceanbulk Shipping & Trading S.A.. (This Order was sealed in envelope #2 and unsealed with Order #4.)(jfe) (Entered: 02/22/2010)
12/04/2010	11	ORDER OF DISMISSAL FILED UNDER SEAL: It is hereby ordered that this action shall be dismissed without prejudice. It is further ordered that this matter shall remain sealed. It is further Ordered that each party shall bear its own costs and fees. (Signed by Judge Victor Marrero on 7/11/2008) (This Order was sealed in envelope #3 and unsealed with Order #4.) (jfe) (Entered: 02/22/2010)

PACER Service Center

LCH FREIGHT VOLUME

VOLUME BY CLIENT

CLIENT	VOLUME 2007	VOLUME 2008 YTD	TOTAL VOLUME 2007-2008	2008 YTD VOL AS % of TOTAL 2007 VOL
OSG	0	270	270	0
MUR SHIPPING	0	45	45	0
OLDENDORFF	23,837	9,584	33,421	40.21
GOLDEN OCEAN	6,526	3,099	9,625	47.49
TMT	25,275	13,302	38,577	52.63
HOUSE	54,912	20,140	75,052	36.68
TOTAL	110,550	46,440	156,990	42.01

RBS VS MARKET VOLUME

MONTH & YEAR	MARKET CLEARED VOLUME	RBS VOLUMES	RBS VOLUMES AS % OF MARKET VOLUMES	RBS FREIGHT MARKET RANKING
NOV'07	100,266	38,322	38.22	1ST
DEC '07	42,221	8,916	21.12	2ND
JAN '08	118,015	28,085	23.80	2ND
FEB '08	73,888	20,885	28.27	2ND

BREAKDOWN BY CONTRACT FOR RBS: 2007 - CURRENT

CONTRACT	VOLUME	% OF TOTAL RBS VOLUME
C4	1,850	1.18
C4E	1,655	1.05
CTC	42,503	27.07
HTC	726	0.46
PTC	71,562	45.58
STC	10,859	6.92
P2A	480	0.31
P3A	350	0.22
TD3	22,425	14.28
TD5	690	0.44
TD7	3,890	2.48
TOTAL	156,990	100.00

BIBLIOGRAPHY

"Bankers To Have Bonuses Clawed Back For 'Inappropriate Behaviour' Under Labour Government" (*Huffington Post* February 13, 2015)

Barofsky, Neil, *Bailout* (Free Press 2012)

Bernanke, Ben, *The Courage To Act* (Norton 2015)

Brown, Gordon, *My Life, Our Times* (Bodley Head 2017)

Business Action Group—RBS GRG, www.rbs-grgbusinessactiongroup.org

BuzzFeedNews, "The Dash For Cash: Leaked Files Reveal RBS Systematically Crushed British Businesses For Profit" (*BuzzFeed*, October 10, 2016)

Chaitman, Helen Davis and Lance Gotthoffer, *JPMadoff: The Unholy Alliance Between America's Biggest Bank and America's Biggest Crook* (Creatspace Independent Publishing Platform 2016)

Chasing Madoff (Cohen Media 2010)

Clark, Andrew, "How the Collapse of Lehman Brothers Pushed Capitalism to the Brink" (*The Guardian*, September 4, 2009)

Cohan, William D, "How Goldman Killed AIG" (*The New York Times*, February 16, 2011)

"Dodd says JPMorgan loss proof of legislation need" (*Reuters*, May 31, 2012)

Ferguson, Charles, *Inside Job* (Sony Pictures 2010)

Financial Crisis Inquiry Commission (US Government Publishing Office), https://www.gpo.gov/fdsys/pkg/GPO-FCIC/pdf/GPO-FCIC.pdf

Financial Times, "The End of Lehman Brothers" (*Financial Times Visual Journalism*, September 17, 2008)

Firger, Jessica, "How Hormones Influence the Stock Market" (*Newsweek* July 6, 2015)

Fishman, Steve, "Burning Down His House" (*New York Magazine*, November 30, 2008)

Fraser, Ian, *Shredded: Inside RBS, the Bank that Broke Britain* (Birlinn Ltd [3rd edition] 2016)

Geithner, Tim, "A legacy of financial failure containment—Leo Panitch" (*The Guardian*, January 30, 2013)

Geithner, Timothy F., *Stress Test* (Crown 2014)

Hurley, James, "RBS Stripped Assets of Struggling Firms" (*The Time*s, May 5, 2015)

Lanchester, John, "Bankocracy" (*London Review of Books*, November 5, 2009)

Lehman Brothers, Chapter 11 bankruptcy protection (September 2008), https://www.sec.gov/Archives/edgar/data/806085/000110465908059632/a08-22764_4ex99d1.htm

Lewis, Michael, *The Big Short: Inside the Doomsday Machine* (Penguin 2011)

Loveday, Alison and Dino Paganuzzi, "FCA publishes summary of Skilled Person Report on GRG" (Kennedy's Law LLP, October 31, 2017) http://www.kennedyslaw.com/article/fca-publishes-summary-of-skilled-person-report-on-grg/

Madoff: The Court Documents—*The New York Times*, https://www.nytimes.com/interactive/projects/documents/bernard-madoff-ponzi-scheme-court-documents

Markopolos, Harry, *No One Would Listen* (Wiley 2011)

Martens, Pam and Russ Martens, "Madoff/Whistleblowers/SEC" (*Wall Street On Parade*, February 4, 2016)

Martin, Iain, *Crash Bang Wallop* (Sceptre 2016)

Newsnight (BBC, October 10, 2016)

Paulson, Henry M, Jr, *On The Brink* (Business Plus 2010, 2013)

Permanent Subcommittee on Investigations, *JPMorgan Chase Whale Trades: A Case History of Derivatives Risks and Abuses* (US Senate, March 15, 2013)

Samuelson, Paul, "Wall Street Indexes Predicted Nine Out Of the Last Five Recessions" (*Newsweek* September 19, 1966)

Scuffman, Matt, "Why RBS May Pay Small Firms it Allegedly Ruined" (*Reuters* September 23, 2015)

Senate Banking, Housing & Urban Affairs Committee report (June 13, 2012), im.ft-static.com/content/images/b87b2a22-b4ce-11e1-aa06-00144feabdc0.pdf

Smith, Greg, *Why I Left Goldman Sachs* (Grand Central Publishing 2012)

Sorkin, Andrew Ross, *Too Big To Fail* (Penguin Books [updated] 2010)

Stewart, James B, "Eight Days" (*The New Yorker*, September 21, 2009)

Sweeney, John, "Mining Giant Glencore Accused in Child Labour Row" (*The Guardian*, April 14, 2012)

Tennyson, Lord Alfred, *In Memoriam A.H.H.* (1849)

The Madoff Recovery Initiative—August 4, 2017, www.madofftrustee.com

The Wizard of Lies (HBO/Tribeca Productions, June 2017)

ILLUSTRATIONS

Milton Keynes UK
Ingram Content Group UK Ltd.
UKHW021531050124
435333UK00007B/15

9 781738 454419